JOURNEY OF A LIFETIME

Alan Whicker

WINDSOR
PARAGON

First published 2009
by HarperCollins*Publishers*
This Large Print edition published 2010
by BBC Audiobooks Ltd
by arrangement with
HarperCollinsPublishers

Hardcover ISBN: 978 1 408 46118 1
Softcover ISBN: 978 1 408 46119 8

British Library Cataloguing in Publication Data available

Printed and bound in Great Britain by
CPI Antony Rowe, Chippenham and Eastbourne

For Valerie, of course—who retraced every step
with me and made each one happy …

And for our friends Anne and David Crossland
who joined this kaleidoscope of Whickerwork
and spread a lot of happiness we were often
lucky enough to share.

CONTENTS

UNKNOWN PLACES FIT FOR
EAGLES AND ANGELS

My first television programme fifty-two years ago involved travel. With a BBC crew of three we struck out for the Near East, and this book recalls the filming of the earliest *Journey of a Lifetime*. The excitement was intense. Nothing daunted, we arrived in . . . *Ramsgate*. Yes, we were considering the livelihood of seaside landladies. Well you have to start somewhere, and they were unflinching.

Mrs Evelyn Stone's poodle Candy wore a new blue and red coat for the occasion, I recall. Opposite us, overlooking the sea, a sight which surely dates the picture—not to mention me. Across the road in Nelson Crescent, a *blitzed* building: roofless and desolate.

Now the BBC has asked me to join in this celebration of my first half-century in television with a memory of some thirty *Journeys of a Lifetime*—a look at the fun, shock and jubilation of half a century spent getting to know interesting people living unusual lives around the world.

The first long-cut of *any* television film is exciting, the second alarming—for you see and hear where you went wrong. To make the first cut the Editor and Director will have removed the humour, to make room. Jokes are *always* the first to go. Editors suspect that they take us away from the storyline, or hold up the action. Unfortunately they also take with them much of the elusive flavour we were chasing—our attitude towards the rest of the world.

Then, gradually, later versions of *Whicker's World* emerge from the cutting rooms and into my study. Everything slowly comes together, from the first interview to the last frame, which is when we start to believe we've caught something special on the screen, whether it's a person, a place or a moment in time. Once we've unlocked the flavour and texture of some people and places, *Whicker's World* goes on turning.

Norfolk Island was just such a place, where I first caught islanditis. This pursued me around the world to such an extent that I left a desirable home in the heart of London and went to live on a tiny island in the Atlantic where I knew no one. I had been travelling all my life and was then living happily in a Nash terrace in Regent's Park, and before that on Richmond Green.

The first different reaction I noticed about Norfolk Island was that whenever two cars passed the drivers always waved to each other. At first I thought my driver had a lot of friends and relations, but then I realized that in an isolated isle of 2,000 people he would surely know every driver, even if he had just missed the last one while those sheep were passing.

Norfolk, a reminder of Switzerland with sea, is about as far as you can go in the South Pacific. It floats in tremendous seas somewhere off Australia and New Zealand—a paradise where nothing bites and nothing stings, where they feed the pigs on passion fruit and the sheep on wild peaches.

The descendants of the *Bounty* mutineers came to Norfolk when they outgrew Pitcairn. Its towering pines and little mountains stand amid seascapes of deep blue ocean and white water—

unknown places fit for eagles and angels.

A contained space where people felt they belonged was comforting for anyone enjoying islanditis, but for the big lifestyle picture I did not want to lose contact with my roots or do without relevant newspapers and television, so some thirty-six years ago I reluctantly gave away the South Pacific and Regent's Park and settled in Jersey, the major Channel Island where motorists don't wave much.

Now when I wake in the morning I look towards France across fourteen miles of magnificent seas— sometimes as still and lovely as a turquoise mirror, other days Wagnerian and threatening. Looking along that Normandy coast towards Cherbourg very little has changed, though just out of sight there's Flammanville and evidence of French determination to rely upon nuclear reactors. A worrisome coastline.

Former Jersey resident Victor Hugo called the Channel Islands 'little specks of France fallen into the sea and gobbled up by the English'. I've never regretted surrendering to this uncommon situation, although the £8 air fare to London that greeted us thirty-six years ago is now about £100, and counting.

In my island paradise, into which 100,000 residents are now squeezing themselves, I am living happily ever after. It's a joy to know I shall spend the rest of my days in this tranquil therapeutic island where spring comes a little early, summer seems endless and autumn hangs around.

My last book written here was *Whicker's War,* a look at the conflict in Italy in which the men who fought there seemed anxious to keep it private, as is the way of soldiers. This book, as you now know, has been an examination of the highs and lows of my first fifty years of television life, played out in public.

Some kindly folk have already asked me for another collection of memories, but between you and me I'm not sure I'm good for *another* half-century—not even with the help of my wonderful Valerie . . . but who knows? It's always possible we might meet again in another *Whicker's World*!

1

THERE'S BEEN A CHANGE OF MANAGEMENT

Flying home from Australia is never a happy undertaking; I've tried it every which way—thirty hours non-stop, or peeling off for a night in Singapore or Bangkok, Hong Kong or LA. However you approach it, you face a long haul, rattling with pills. Jet lag always wins.

I'd recommend travel on Christmas Day. Planes are empty, service is great—the stewards have no one else to talk to. Champagne and Anton Mosimann's best puddings seem to taste even better at 32,000 feet—but this time, flying from Haiti, I had been invited to break the journey in Los Angeles and spend the holiday with Cubby Broccoli, granddaddy of James Bond, and his wife Dana—who took an instant dislike to Fagin, as played by Ron Moody.

We had a Californian Christmas: bright sunshine, extravagant presents, interesting company. One day we flew to Las Vegas with that splendid old actor Bruce Cabot—a relative of Cubby's—who had been the lead in *King Kong*. Not much to do with snow and reindeer, but he fitted in beautifully—and the monkey was great.

The day before we left for London, there was a party at the home of Harold Robbins; I'd made a *Whicker's World* around him a few months earlier. Harold could behave very much like a character in one of his novels, but I found him oddly likeable. He could be boorish and boastful—which seems to happen to bestsellers—but then in a complex blend he was courteous and charming in a rather old-fashioned way. He was married at the time to Grace, a darkly attractive woman who seemed able to cope with his erratic lifestyle.

While writing in New York he liked to stay at the Elysée Hotel, a quiet place off Madison Avenue favoured by Tennessee Williams and other authors. We left the Plaza to join him and quickly slipped into the Robbins routine, meeting his stable of available ladies in the evening and drinking good Californian burgundy served at precisely 64 degrees.

'Guess what she does?' he demanded, after introducing a leggy blonde in hot pants. I had a pretty good idea what she might do, but suggested instead a model, an actress, beauty consultant, hair designer, nail technician ... 'No,' he cried, triumphantly. 'She's a *store detective.*'

Her in-store career came to an abrupt end when Harold's publishers conveniently noticed that his latest novel was way behind schedule. She was dispatched to a Spanish holiday on a one-way ticket.

I had been pleased with our programme around Harold, *I'm the World's Best Writer—There's Nothing More to Say.* It had a good story—Hell's Kitchen to Côte d'Azur yachts, by way of one portable typewriter. Interesting locations and an articulate subject who, it later transpired, had a slight problem separating fact from passing fantasy.

Harold's editor Simon was a splendid, articulate man and I was anxious that he should be included in our programme. I broached the subject during a jolly lunch with them both, but to my surprise he

2

refused point blank: 'Didn't you notice how he started breaking up all those table matches while you were talking to me?' Simon was not about to risk upsetting his golden goose for a few minutes' exposure on *Whicker's World*.

Sitting around the Robbins's Beverly Hills pool on that bright December afternoon were old friends from London and the Côte d'Azur, Leslie and Evie Bricusse. Leslie was responsible for some of the great standards of the Sixties and Seventies, often with Anthony Newley. If you hear something familiar, plaintive and lyrical, it's usually Leslie asking 'What kind of fool am I?' or somesuch. At the peak of his career he was now hard at work in Hollywood, hitting high notes for friends Sammy Davis Jr and Frank Sinatra, and *'Talking to the Animals.'*

We had not met for months, and were anxious to catch up. He had been writing the music for *Dr Doolittle*, so we swapped the usual 'Rex Harrison as Producer' horror stories. I told him of my excitement at finally buying a house in Jersey—my first permanent home. He looked alarmed. 'I wouldn't set foot on that island,' he said. 'We'll *never* visit you there.' This seemed surprising, and odd. Jersey is peaceful and off the beaten track for globe-trotting Hollywood winners. How come that fierce reaction?

Leslie had quite rightly become hugely successful. He had a cute wife, Evie, and homes in Mexico, France, London, Malta and Beverly Hills. His income had grown so much that he had been told to restructure his finances. An international lawyer living in the Channel Islands was recommended as his saviour, and a hugely

3

complicated scheme had been hatched with law offices around the world which the Jersey lawyer would administer, and in return for this legal expertise Leslie would pay him 10 per cent of his earnings over a period of ten years. It was that kind of nightmare financial complication that you wish was keeping *you* alive.

A few months after signing that contract the Bricusses began to regret their involvement with this pedantic little Jerseyman. Pages of notes would arrive on a weekly basis suggesting changes to score and libretto. Not unnaturally, Leslie did not take kindly to such improbable interference from an insufferable musical know-all. Stressed out and working hard, he decided he must break the agreement—but found his new legal partner had no intention of releasing him.

Expensive law firms on both sides of the Atlantic were once again consulted. The contract was found to be binding and watertight. To fight it would have taken years and sapped Leslie's creative energy while he was still on his winning streak. He was forced to capitulate. A settlement was reached whereby the Jersey lawyer would instead take 90 per cent of his earnings for one year—and then release him. This was expected to be the year of his greatest successes when all his projects were hits, but he was cleaned out. Frustrated after signing away the fortune he'd spent a lifetime building, the mild and gentle Leslie went home and trashed every breakable object in his house.

Smiling and soft-spoken, he was popular at the studios. Soon everyone had heard of his fury and despair that he had been strangled by the small

4

print. Several friendly groups generously offered to 'sort out' the villain of the piece—that Jersey lawyer. The agreement might have been watertight, but these friends were not smiling all the time.

The local Mafia boss made it known that he would be only too happy to do Leslie a favour and remove any financial blockage, as between men of honour you understand.

The Las Vegas backstage fraternity also offered help in his hour of crisis, which sounded seriously final. As a last graphic decision, there was a group of friendly stunt men from Pinewood who spent their lives being thrown off bridges and fighting each other. They knew the island well, so also hatched a detailed plot to rescue poor Leslie.

The house where the Jersey lawyer lived was on a hilltop above a secluded bay with a perfect view of France, 14 miles away. A forest path snaked up from the sea through the garden and right up to his front door. They could arrive at night by a boat with padded oars, do whatever deed was required while the island—and the lawyer—slept, and steal away. Piece of cake.

I don't think the people at that Beverly Hills party realized life-and-death decisions were being discussed and agreed. While I listened, some of Leslie's friends explained the lie of the land to each other, and I began to realize they were not merely talking about the house—'Lovely position, lovely!'—but my future.

It was *my* new home they were planning to visit that night. 'Perfect for the getaway, that coastline.'

'Listen,' I said, when I got my voice back, 'I've just *bought* that house. I'm planning to live in it for years. Now you're going to *kill* the guy in the main bedroom! That's *me*. Please tell all your friends there's been a change of management.'

2

A TALK WITH SOMEONE
WHO'S NOT TREMBLING

I passed a couple of restless days in Miami—a place quite easy to dislike. I was bracing myself to fly somewhere even worse. *Far* worse. I had just completed a series of *Whicker's World*s in South America. All the fun and excitement of filming in Argentina (brilliant), on to Peru (druggy), then up among the volcanoes outside Quito in Ecuador (enchanting) and finally coming to rest in downtown Miami for a couple of apprehensive days awaiting PanAm's lifeline flight to the kidnap capital of the world: Haiti.

Miami Beach was the place where, waking one morning in a vast white hotel totally surrounded by avarice, I took a taxi to the airport and asked for a ticket to *anywhere*. They thought I was mad—and probably by then I was, a little.

Now—ice-cold sane—I was approaching a *far* more dangerous destination: Haiti. The first black republic was only some 700 miles away, but its reputation made trigger-happy Floridians seem cool and chummy. This poorest country in the Western hemisphere survives with 80 per cent of its population below the poverty line.

I was on my reluctant way to examine Papa Doc's

republic—and Papa Doc, I had heard, was about to examine *me*. Not everyone walked away from those check-ups, our pilot told me cheerfully. In the world's kidnap centre the dungeons were active, with Papa Doc as a frequent spectator.

Our jet, not surprisingly, was almost empty. It was a good plane to miss. We flew across the fringe of the Sargasso Sea, which seemed a suitable setting for any adventure, landed at François Duvalier Airport in Port-au-Prince, and drew breath. So far, so still alive.

This despairing nation was under the lash of a President for Life whose years of absolute power had brought terror to his people and ruin to his country. As I walked through the damp heat towards the decrepit arrivals building I saw, seared across the peeling white plaster of the wall that confronted me, a pockmarked line of bullet holes.

This was a fairly emphatic take-it-or-leave-it statement. It didn't say whether it was a gesture from the Tourist Division of the Chamber of Commerce, but it was surely more arresting than the traditional view of Port-au-Prince from the mountains. It was the only airport welcome Haiti offered its rare visitors, and it was right in character.

Inside the building, a more friendly reception from the President's official greeter, Aubelin Jolicœur. This small, unctuous executive silenced the customs men who had scented rich pickings from us with a wave of his ivory-handled cane. I recognized him instantly: he had been drawn to perfection as Petit Pierre in Graham Greene's frightening *The Comedians.*

He may have been smiling, but the Haitians

watching us in the arrivals hall were expressionless, which suggested he wasn't all *that* funny. Tontons Macoutes no longer stripped or frisked arrivals, though I was uncomfortably aware that the airport had just experienced one of those dramatic bloodlettings which would have seemed improbable fiction from Graham Greene.

The eldest of Dr Duvalier's three daughters, his favourite Marie-Denise, had just married the 6'3' Commander of his Palace Guard, Captain Max Dominique, who instantly became a Colonel. Then Papa Doc, acting upon different advice, decided his new son-in-law was involved in the plot against him for which he had just executed nineteen brother-officers.

Having considered the pleas of his wife and daughter, then pregnant, he spared Col. Dominique, but sent him into exile and out of the way as ambassador to Spain. As they left for Madrid, the President and Mrs Duvalier came to the airport to bid a sorrowful farewell to Di-Di.

For the traditional VIP goodbye picture the young couple stood at the aircraft door, waving to parents, friends and staff. As the door was closing upon the happy couple, there came a nod from Papa Doc. Their chauffeur and two bodyguards were shot down in front of them. Dr Duvalier was making his own farewell gesture of disapproval.

He turned and left the bloodstained tarmac without another glance at the dying men. They lay in the sunlight under the eyes of the few horrified passengers *en route* from Miami to Puerto Rico. The aircraft then departed abruptly. An American airman who had seen it all told me, 'That captain practically took off with the door open. They just wanted to get *out* of there.'

There were no further executions on the evening of our arrival, but the scarred walls were adequate reminders. Outside we were distributed among waiting taxi drivers. They were all Tontons Macoutes, Papa Doc's private army licensed to extort. Driving a cab was the best-paid job in the land at the time—the only one in which a Haitian could get his hands on foreign currency.

My personal Tonton was silent and sinister, with a Gauguin face. He had the poetic name of Racine. He also had red eyes.

There was no question of hotel selection; you went and lived where you were put. Racine drove us skilfully through the bumps and up the hillside to the white concrete Castelhaiti Hotel, overlooking the town. It was empty—but ready for us.

That evening ours was the only occupied table as we tackled some stringy chicken. Groups of listless waiters stood around in the gloom, watching and whispering while a piano and violin wailed mournfully in the shadows. Outside the fearful town, hushed and tense, awaited its regular power cut.

My crew soon gave up, and went to sort their equipment. It was jollier. We had called the camera for tomorrow and would find something to shoot. We needed to establish contact with the inaccessible Papa Doc. 'Once we've been seen with him, talking to him, we'll be all right,' said my Australian researcher, Ted Morrisby, who as usual had tuned in cleverly. 'Then the Tontons and the rest of the town will know he accepts us. That means we shan't get hassled, or shot.'

9

Well, he convinced *me*. In a land where we had no friends for protection, no embassy to turn to, there was a convincing argument for establishing contact before any more shots rang out.

Certainly Papa Doc was not easy to reach. His massacres had generated terror and despair and hidden fury, so every day he prepared to face some sort of counter-attack. He rarely left the white American-built National Palace, the only important building in town which could be instantly switched into a floodlit armed fortress, yet he did not feel secure even behind its walls and guarded gates.

The President had ousted Paul Magloire, who had twice sent in old B25 aircraft on bombing runs. The grounds were ringed by anti-aircraft guns and elderly armoured cars. The President also beseeched protection from a new prayer of which he was author. He sought support from all sides:

Our Doc, who art in the National Palace for Life,
Hallowed be thy name, by present and future
   generations
Thy will be done at Port-au-Prince and in the
   provinces.
Give us this day our new Haiti and never forgive
   the trespasses of the anti-patriots . . .

By a stroke of Whicker's luck we discovered that next day Our Doc was making a rare expedition into the anxious surroundings outside his palace. He was to open a new Red Cross centre, a small building a few hundred yards from his fortress.

We left our silent hotel at dawn and reached the area as troops and armed men began to assemble

10

for the ceremony. There were hundreds of soldiers in well-pressed khaki with medals and white gloves, and of course a lot of armament. Militia wore blue denim with a red stripe for the occasion, like army hospital patients; more guns, of course. Mingling with authority among them were men in thin tight suits,snap-brimmed fedoras and shades, like Mods heading for Brighton Beach and waving light automatics around casually: the Tontons.

As usual when overwhelmed by armed men enjoying a little brief authority, I adopted an attitude of polite preoccupied condescension—like a prefect moving down upon a third-former whose mother is hovering. For a new and meaningful relationship with an unwelcoming armed guard, it helps to be slightly patronizing but brandishing a permanent smile. It also helps if you're saying something like, 'Do you mind standing aside, *please*. British television filming the President. Thank you so much, just back a bit more . . .' He doesn't understand, but he gets your drift and suspects you might be Somebody, or know Somebody.

It is hard to shoot a man, or even strike him with your rifle butt, when he is smiling at you in a friendly way and talking about something foreign. It helps the odds.

The confident, cheerful attitude won through again. When they expect you to be humble and timid, a certain pleasant senior-officer asperity throws them off-balance. This is even more effective when guards or police or hoodlums don't understand English.

To attempt their language, whatever it is, instantly places you in the subordinate position of supplication, and invites questions. Since adopting this haughty approach, I am pleased to say I've hardly ever been shot.

So we stood in the searing sunshine in what seemed like a sharpshooters' convention, waiting for Papa. I became aware that one or two of the more heavily armed men had started talking about us and doubtless about our presence as interlopers upon their scene. Before they could get their little brief authority together, there was a distant roar of massed motorcycles.

The first arrival was, improbably, a chromium-plated Harley-Davidson, ridden by a large black dressed like a tubby boy scout. On his pillion was a younger man in a sort of beach gear. Presumably they were significant figures, but they didn't seem to threaten my prefect, who was at that moment telling senior spectators to move back a bit to allow better pictures.

They were followed at a distance by a horde of regulation military outriders surrounding an enormous black Mercedes 600. This noisy group had come at least 600 yards from the palace gates. The limo stopped. A sort of tremor ran through the massed troops.

A couple of portly colonels with machine guns struggled out and stood to attention, quivering. After a long pause, a small stooped figure in a dark suit emerged, with a white frizz under his black homburg. Blinking behind thick lenses in the sudden silence, he asked in a whisper for what appeared to be the Mace of Haiti: the President's own sub-machine gun. This was handed to him and, reassured, he restored it to a guard. His gestures were those of fragile old age, and he walked with a slight shuffle; yet this was the man who held a nation by the throat.

He noticed our white faces and camera instantly, but without acknowledgement. He had presumably been alerted by Joliecœur. After military salutes and anthems, he entered the small Red Cross building with his wife, Mme Simone Ovide Duvalier, a handsome Creole in a large white hat, closely followed by me, as usual brushing machine guns aside with a polite smile and a '*So* sorry, do you mind?'

In the scrimmage Ted Morrisby and I managed to converge upon the President. In a way we were expected. We explained we had crossed the world to see him for an important programme, and after some hesitant queries received a murmured invitation to visit his palace next day. We fell back with relief from the small figure who seemed to wish us no harm.

Later we learned that his chargé d'affaires in London was a *Whicker's World* enthusiast, and upon our request for visas had sent Papa Doc an approving telex.

Coming to power in 1957 with the support of the army, the astute Dr Duvalier had observed that dictators were always overthrown by their own armies—usually the Commander of the Presidential Guard—so he overthrew his, quite quickly.

He explained his military philosophy to me later, in an angry rasp: 'Only civilians can own a country, not the military men. The military man must stay in his barracks and receive orders and instructions from the President, from the King, fromthe Emperor. This is my opinion, this is my philosophy. To have peace and stability you must have a strong man in every country.'

'A dictator?' I suggested. The hesitant soft voice rasped again: 'Not a dictator, a *strong* man! Democracy is only a word—it is a philosophy, a conception. What you call democracy in your country, another country might call dictatorship.'

His Haitian army once had 20,000 men—6,500 of them generals. It was now reduced to ceremonial duties, and colonels. In its place the President created his Volunteers for Defence—the evil militia of Tontons Macoutes. This unthreatening phrase meant 'Uncle Bagman' after the legendary giant bogeyman who strode the mountains stuffing naughty children into his knapsack.

In return for loyalty, Duvalier gave his army bully boys the right to lean upon the terrified populace, to tax and torment. Every nationalized hoodlum performed discipline duties with which Papa Doc did not wish to be publicly associated, and was licensed to kill. To provoke or deny any bogeyman intent upon stuffing his knapsack was to invite a beating, at least.

All hope drained from the nation during Duvalier's years of sudden and unaccountable death, as Haitians submitted to the gangster army which stood over them, controlled improbably by Mme Rosalee Adolph, Deputy, wife of the Minister of Health and Population, who had since 1958 been the Supervisor General of the Volunteers: 'They are not paid—though I am paid, because I am a Deputy. If we are attacked someone has to defend the Head of Government. I have always got my gun. It is always ready.'

The smiling little woman packed it, demurely, in

14

her handbag. After she had proved her firepower we all went, obligingly, up a mountainside to see some of her volunteers in action. We had expected a mass of toiling figures but found only a handful working on a road, watched by twice as many whose duty, it seemed, was to watch. Tontons did not volunteer to work—they volunteered to supervise.

By then Papa Doc was believed to have executed 2,000 Haitians and driven 30,000 into exile and the rest into terrified silence. In that manacled land it seemed unlikely that there was anyone left to criticize, let alone attack. A missing Haitian would be unimportant and unnoticed, though the arrest or death of a foreigner could only be ordered by the President. There was little comfort in that, for he seemed totally unconcerned about international criticism.

A foreign passport was no protection. The Dominican consul was found with his throat slashed so ferociously that his head was almost severed. Cromwell James, a 61-year-old British shop owner, was arrested by Tontons and severely beaten—presumably for resisting extortion. It took ten days for his lawyer to reach him in jail, to find he had been charged with highway robbery! He died four days later: gangrene, from untreated wounds.

In a destitute land, such extortion yielded diminishing returns, for there were always fewer victims to be squeezed. When the Tontons began to demand money from foreigners the British Ambassador, Gerald Corley-Smith, complained. He was thrown out and the embassy closed. Duvalier renounced the convention of political

15

asylum and raided other embassies to get at terrified Haitians hiding from the Tontons. Washington was curtly told to recall its ambassador, Raymond Thurston—who was Papa Doc's financial crutch.

Though Haiti was officially Catholic, the church was also attacked. Archbishop Raymond Poirier was arrested and put on a Miami flight wearing a cassock and sash and carrying one dollar. Soon after his successor, the Haitian Bishop Augustus, was dragged from his bed by Tontons and not even allowed to put in his false teeth before he was deported. The Catholic Bishop and eighteen Jesuit priests followed him, as did the American Episcopal Bishop Alfred Voegeli, who had ministered to Haitians for twenty years. Papa Doc accepted the Pope's excommunication with his usual equanimity and went on to ban the Boy Scouts.

Next year President Johnson agreed to send another ambassador to Port-au-Prince, Mr Benson Timmons III. Papa Doc kept him waiting five weeks for an audience, and then gave him a stern lecture on how a diplomat should behave.

Committing international hara-kiri, antagonizing the world while continuing to ask for aid, may not have made economic sense, but to Haitians it made some emotional sense: proud Haiti, first to defy the slave master, once again standing alone. From their point of view Dr Duvalier had one vital thing going for him: most of Haiti's presidents had been upper-class mulattoes with light skins, but Papa Doc was as black as his hat.

In the years following the war some hundreds of millions of dollars were given or loaned to this friendless nation, much of it going directly to President Duvalier. The world finally realized Haiti was too corrupt and hopeless to help, so the dollars dried up. When we arrived in December 1968 the economy was in a state of collapse—finance in chaos, public works decaying, few passable roads and a government so venal that all trade not offering corrupt officials a rake-off was at a standstill.

With the lowest income, food intake and life expectancy in the hemisphere, the lives of the amiable, long-suffering Haitians have changed little since the days of slavery two centuries ago. Shoes are still a luxury. I found it impossible to exaggerate the poverty of a land so out of step with the rest of the world. From a workforce of two or three million, only 60,000 had jobs—almost all on the government payroll.

There seemed little chance of strikes. The unemployed had heard the President's personal physician Dr Jacques Fourcand warn what would happen if Haiti ever found the energy to rise against Papa Doc: 'Blood will flow as never before. The land will burn. There will be no sunrise and no sunset—just one enormous flame licking the sky. It will be the greatest slaughter in history—a Himalaya of corpses.' That benevolent doctor was a neurosurgeon and President of the local Red Cross, when not attending to the Father of the Nation.

Fear and violence were not new to that fevered land where the cheapest possession had always been life. It was once the richest French colony, but after the only successful slave revolt, in 1804, suffered a succession of tyrannical black

17

governors, emperors and kings. In half a century there were sixty-nine violent revolutions. They left behind the world's poorest country—a mountainous, teeming tropical land, only twice the size of Yorkshire. Nine out of ten of the 5 million Haitians are illiterate, but they are a sympathetic and artistic people, the women docile and, it was said, like panthers dreaming.

My only pleasure in that cowed capital came from the *Peintres Naïfs*. I was particularly taken with Préfet Duffaut, a sort of Haitian Lowry who always painted his native village of Jacmel and peopled it with busy matchstick figures. I bought two of his paintings and later gave the better one to my friend, the lovely Cubby Broccoli who was my Christmas host later that month in Beverly Hills. I realized on arrival at Cubby's new home that the simple, charming primitive painting was quite out of place in his grand new mansion off Sunset Boulevard, and was surely destined to rest in one of his distant loos. I longed to ask for it back in exchange for something more suitable— say, a Rubens.

For any foreigner not affected by poverty or tyranny, Haiti still provided a dramatic holiday background. In those stricken days one cruise ship arrived each week from Miami. This stayed only a few hours, as most of the passengers were too frightened to go ashore.

To tidy up the foreground for the adventurous, all beggars were banished to the countryside for the day. Jealous Tontons stood watching for the braver to file ashore and fill their predatory line of elderly taxis. They were then driven up the lowering mountainside behind the capital to the

18

little resort of Kenscoff, where they watched some flaming limbo dancers across their cold buffets before returning with relief to their ship, and sailing away.

We recorded their sad celebration amid despair, but left early to be ready to film the dockside departure. As we drove down the mountain, there in the middle of the road was a brand new corpse, still bleeding.

The unfortunate man was obviously dead. A body asleep, drunk or just unconscious is somehow ... different. I told Racine to stop so that we could go back and at least cover the poor chap. He refused, and drove on faster. No Haitian would ever touch or rearrange any Tontons' handwork for fear of suffering the same fate. That was why those bullet-scars across the airport walls had been left uncovered.

So all the cruise passengers in their motorcade which followed us down the mountain had to drive solemnly and in procession around that corpse. What the blue rinses from Pasadena made of this holiday demonstration I cannot imagine, but it surely did nothing for the Tourist Board's 'Come to Happy Haiti' promotion.

Haitians have seldom been able to summon up more energy for imported Christianity than was required to bury their dead, Tontons permitting. They may be 90 per cent Catholic, as the reference books say, but they are 100 per cent voodoo. In Haiti the supernatural is still alive.

When a peasant dies, before being placed in his coffin he may be dressed in his best clothes—if he has any—and seated at a table with food and a lighted cigarette between his lips or, if a woman, a

19

clay pipe. When friends and neighbours arrive the feasting and dancing of the wake begins. Although by law the corpse is supposed to be buried within twenty-four hours, decomposition is often allowed to set in. This ensures that sorcerers will not dig him up and make a zombie, a work slave, out of him. The heavy stone slabs with which Haitians cover their graves are added insurance that the dead will not rise to slave as zombies for the rest of time.

Papa Doc angrily denied to me that he was a *houngan*, a voodoo priest—or even a follower of Baron Samedi, the most powerful and dreaded god in the voodoo pantheon. Baron Samedi personified death itself. He was always dressed in black and wore dark glasses. The President's choice of wardrobe may not have been accidental.

In 1963 President Duvalier received information that one of his few political opponents still alive, Clément Barbot, a former Commander of the Tontons Macoutes but now in hiding, had transformed himself into a black dog. Papa Doc quickly ordered that all black dogs in Haiti should be killed. Barbot was later captured and shot to death by Tontons; he was still a man.

Certainly there were many stories about the brutal President, some terrible, some silly. It was said that he sought guidance from the entrails of goats, that he lay meditating in his bath wearing his black hat; that he had the head of one of his few enemies still about, Captain Blucher Philogènes, delivered to him in a pail of ice. He then sat for hours trying to induce the head to disclose the plotters' plans . . .

He was merciless, despotic, malign; yet he

received me in his study with eerie amiability. Behind him were signed portraits of the men he admired: Chiang Kai-Shek, President Lyndon Johnson, the Pope and Martin Luther King.

He told me he blamed the world-wide loathing he had earned on an 'international conspiracy set up by several white nations who spent many millions of dollars to destroy our Fatherland, sending the North American 6th Fleet to violate our national sea'.

He then muttered darkly, 'The USA has been sending *un*capable ambassadors so there is no talk between them and the President of Haiti. It is a question of men. The FBI is doing a good job, but the CIA not. It makes much trouble and must be blamed for the bad impression the world has of my country.'

He dismissed the insurgents' bombing of his palace: 'They are crazy. They will never reach their aim because I know who I am and I can't be killed by anyone. I have faith in my destiny. No other President of Haiti could stand up and do what I did in the past eleven years—facing eight armed invasions and three hurricanes.'

Though he was President for Life and apparently convinced of his immortality, I wondered whether he had thought of a successor. He had not. 'All of them are at school now—they are the young people.'

His only son Jean-Claude was sitting beside us in the presidential study. What he would do with his life? The fat moon-faced 17-year-old was embarrassed. 'That depends on him,' said Papa Doc, regarding his son with pride. 'I hope he will follow the advice of his father, of his mother, and

21

become a medical doctor.'

As I grew more familiar with the President, I became more convinced that nobody's all good or all bad. He had been a mild little country doctor looking after the peasants and earning his famous nickname. This non-smoking teetotaller who loved his family now saw himself as a poet. He presented me with Copy No. 892 of his *Breviaries of a Revolution,* and inscribed a collection of his poems, *Souvenirs d'Autrefois,* 'to a friend of the first Black Revolution, Mr Alan Whicker, in souvenir of his short stay in the Island of Quisquetya, Sincerely, François Duvalier'.

It was said that after dinner in his palace he would sometimes go down to the dungeons to watch some political prisoners tortured, and on occasion might torture them himself. He was certainly known to slap ministers around his study, under the protective gaze of the Presidential Guard. A man of moods, he was sometimes almost playful and anxious to make a good impression, then glowering with suppressed fury at a critical word.

I had played myself in tactfully while getting to know him, leaving the tougher questions for a later visit. Then half-way through one conversation, I caught him regarding me balefully during a long silence. With a low menacing rasp, he said, 'Mr Whicker, you are talking to the President of the Republic of Haiti.' It seemed a telling rebuke.

My crew had caught the distant clang of cell doors slamming, so when I turned to less sensitive matters there were audible sighs of relief from behind the camera. On a following day I reverted to my critical questions, about which he was matter-of-fact. It seemed that his occasional moods might be medically induced.

On one of these jollier days he even decided to show us his capital—and certainly one of the best views of Port-au-Prince had to be from the President's bullet-proof Mercedes 600 limousine.

Papa Doc settled on the back seat alongside his gloomy bodyguard, Col. Gracia Jacques. We had no radio mikes in those days so our recordist Terry Ricketts rigged the unprotesting President with a neck mike and a long lead hidden around his body. Upon jumping out of the limo he several times did himself a slight injury, but without complaint.

He obviously wanted to show how popular he was, and certainly knew how to attract and hold an audience. A breathless cheering crowd chased us as we drove slowly through the town. Then I noticed Papa Doc was throwing handfuls of money out of his window. Our pursuers, scrambling in the dirt, were going frantic. When we stopped the President increased the excitement by bringing out packets of brand-new notes, peeling off wads and handing them out to anyone who seemed to have the right attitude.

In this land of destitution, the arrival of the black Mercedes amid a shower of free banknotes caused far more ecstasy than Santa Claus. With an annual income in every crisp wad handed out, it was well worth trying to keep up with the Duvaliers.

It seemed unreal to be riding around with one of the world's most feared men, discussing subjects none of his countrymen would dare *think*. I asked how he felt about Graham Greene and *The Comedians*. He brushed the novel and the gory film aside. 'He is a poor man, mentally, because he did not say the truth about Haiti. Perhaps he needed the money, and got some from the political exiles.'

He was far more bitter about a predecessor, Major Magloire, then living in New York but threatening to return, because *he* had got away with the money: 'He took $19 million from the National Bank of Haiti and used this money to finance armed invasions and to bomb the palace. He tried to kill me when he was president. I was in hiding for several years. Why did he not come here himself instead of sending his young officers?'

He answered that one himself, right away: 'If he comes here he will be killed, because he is what you call a vagabond. A vagabond.'

Almost half of Haiti's revenue was spent on Papa Doc's personal security. So I questioned the use of his hated Tontons Macoutes: 'It is a militia, they help me to clean the streets, they help me to cultivate the land, they help the Haitian army and they fight side by side in face of armed invasions.' Papa Doc got out of the limo, and the escort of Tontons instantly set up defensive positions around us, as though assassination was imminent.

He could not understand why he was dreaded by so many of his people: 'I am the strongest man, the most anti-Communist man in the Caribbean islands. Certainly the question is a racial one because I am a strong leader. The US considers me a bad example for the 25 million Negroes living there. I should be the favourite child of the United States,' he said, stumbling in his enthusiasm for the subject. 'Instead of which they consider me . . . the black sheep!' He gave me our programme title—a cackle, and one of those ghoulish grins.

Although his 500-strong Palace Guard now recognized us and knew we were harmless and acceptable, they were all permanently terrified of doing anything new, like allowing us through the wrong door. Getting in to see him was a daily problem.

I had the forethought to arm myself with a pass sternly addressed to 'All Civil and Military Authorities' and signed by the President himself. This got me through the sentries on the palace gate, past a quiver of anxious guards on various doors, up the stairs and along the corridor and right up to the entrance to his chambers. There I was stopped by the Presidential Guard itself, a nervous group of captains and lieutenants who admitted they knew he was expecting me, but had no authority to disturb him. This was the Haitian 'Catch-22'.

The only person who could actually approach him was his secretary, Mme Saint-Victor, a formidable lady and sister of another son-in-law—but she was away ill. So we sat under the chandelier in his annex while the President sat inside and waited, and nobody had the determination to knock on his door.

In exasperation I finally broke the stalemate by leaving the palace and going to the town's telegraph office. I had seen a telex in Papa Doc's inner sanctum and noted the number—3490068—so sent a message: 'Mr President, I am waiting outside your door.' This worked.

Encouraged by our successful tour of the town, I suggested he might show us Duvalierville, which he ordered built several years ago as a national showplace, a sort of governmental Brasilia which would be his memorial. He said it was 20 miles away, and that was too far for him to travel. He was always most cautious when on the open road.

We later went to look for ourselves and found he was not missing much. Like everything else in Haiti, his empty dream had died for lack of finance. Crumbling and overgrown, the few piles of cracking white concrete stood in wasteland populated by a few listless squatters. It seemed a fitting monument. However, the President agreed to organize a visit to a nearby health centre. I listened as on one of the few working telephones in the land he chased his daughter to become an extra: 'C'est le President de la République! Where is Di-Di?'

A stoic health centre patient with hepatitis had been organized to be looked at by Papa Doc, so now he would not *dare* to die. Across the body I recalled that the President was still a Fellow of the Royal Society of Tropical Medicine in London. He was delighted. 'Do you know that? Yes, I am surprising, eh? I am still interested in medical matters and until I die I am just an MD and after that President of Haiti. It was the best time of my life, when I was practising medicine.'

I wondered what he now did for relaxation. 'My reading and writing, because this is another aspect of Dr Duvalier. He is a writer and a reader. Even when I am going to sleep I have a book in my hand. This is morphine for me. If I do not read I cannot sleep.' Sometimes he was a hard man to dislike.

I had established an unusual relationship with him, and on occasion I could even make him laugh. Despite the fact that I was persuading the

26

grim but courteous Papa Doc to speak English—
he was far more comfortable with French or
Creole—it seemed he was beginning to enjoy a
conversation with someone who was not trembling.

Ambassadors and archbishops expelled,
ministers sacked, critics shot, yet television
entertained and hostile questioning accepted . . . A
strange world.

It was getting stranger, for we were running out
of film. We had already shot programmes in
Argentina, Paraguay and Ecuador, and our
messages calling for the dispatch of further film
stock were growing more urgent. Yorkshire
Television had only been running a few months
and was still not quite sure what owning a major
television centre was all about. Our cables were
ignored because it was a weekend, and Christmas
was approaching.

When stock was eventually dispatched from
Leeds it was not sent directly to Jamaica, our
neighbouring island, but via PanAm's notorious
Cargo section in New York where, as we feared, it
disappeared from sight.

Filming, however, was going brilliantly. All we
needed for our documentary was a climax, and we
got that when Papa Doc told me that next day he
was going Christmas shopping with Mme Duvalier
and Di-Di, and would I like to film the expedition?
When presidents start suggesting their own
sequences, even I begin to feel quietly confident.
The prospect of the terrifying dictator taking our
film crew shopping around his capital was like a
skeleton in a paper hat: macabre, but fascinating.
It had to be the televisory situation of a lifetime.

My crew sensed an award-winning programme.

This reconciled us wonderfully to the gloom and anxiety, the inedible food and the unpredictable presidential moods, the constant fear that at any moment something could go fatally wrong—and no one would hear a cry for help.

At that moment we ran out of film.

This presented endless new problems. As I had discovered with General Alfredo Stroessner of Paraguay, filming a dictator who does not want to be filmed can be quite dangerous. What is even more fatal, however, is *not* filming a dictator who *wants* to be filmed. He is not used to arguments or excuses or sweet reason. Dictators can only dictate.

Back at the hotel we had a despairing conference around empty camera magazines. What to do? One way or another he was going to be displeased. This could lead to a sudden restriction of liberty—or even a spilling of blood.

We could hardly say we were not interested any more, thank you, Mr President. We could not stand him up, or we might be escorted downstairs to the dungeons. We could not leave the country without an exit visa—and anyway our movements were followed by scores of eyes.

We had been anxious to establish a relationship, but now it seemed, to my surprise, that one could get *too* close to a dictator.

On the morning of our Christmas present expedition I was half hoping the guards outside the palace would hold us up again, even more firmly, but of course for the first time we were swept straight in, with salutes. So I handed my cameraman Frank Pocklington the small pocket camera I used, a little half-frame Olympus Pen F,

28

and went on to spend the morning chatting with a marvellously relaxed President in various jewellers' shops while my cameraman took happy-snaps, in anguish. For a documentary it was a dream situation—except that our cameraman was taking despairing paparazzi pictures, incredulous at what he was missing.

Papa Doc did not notice the absence of our Arriflex, of course. He was far too busy selecting the best jewellery he could find in the guarded shops, while behind him his womenfolk went through the stock with shrewd and practised eyes. I watched Di-Di riffle through a boxful of diamonds; she was surely a chip off the Old Doc.

As our presidential cortège arrived, each jeweller's face became a study: on one hand, it was a great honour to be 'By Appointment' to Dr Duvalier. Such presidential approval had all sorts of side benefits, like the Tontons did not kill you. On the other hand there was one slight but unavoidable snag: he never *paid* for anything.

He would make his selections with much care and then, instead of handing over his credit card, would shake the shopkeeper's hand and award him a wolfish smile. He got a few wolfish smiles back, as though the jeweller was going down for the third time, but there was nothing they could do. At least he only took one item from each shop, and, knowing the gift you carry gets home first, Papa Doc always carried his with him, gift-wrapped, when he left. No exchanges required.

Back in our gloomy hotel, beyond caring and defeated by a distant delivery system, we booked seats on the next flight out to Miami. We had not exposed a foot of film on that unreal and unrepeatable scene. It was lost, along with the remainder of our planned programme climax. Papa Doc had been spared my most pointed questions, which I was thoughtfully withholding for the night before we flew away.

For despair and frustration it was my worst television experience. I went back to the palace to say my farewells, tackling the succession of sentries for the last time.

Yorkshire twice transmitted our programme, *Papa Doc—The Black Sheep*. It was later shown several times by ITV, and submitted by our Controller, Donald Baverstock, for the Dumont Award. This international accolade for television journalism was presented by the University of California and the West Coast philanthropist Nat Dumont. Among the heavyweight judges were the United Nations Undersecretary General, Dr Ralph Bunche, Mrs Katharine Graham, owner of the *Washington Post,* and George Stevens Jr, Director of the American Film Institute. There were 400 entries and 40 finalists.

Papa Doc won.

*   *   *

The runner-up for this prestigious award was a film by Austrian Television which dealt with the US Strategic Air Force. The awards merited stern West Coast editorials complaining that foreign stations had walked away with US television's main prizes. The *Los Angeles Times* said, 'What is ironic is not only that foreign television is beating us at our own game—but with our own stories.'

I flew to Los Angeles for the ceremony, where

the University's Melnitz auditorium was crammed with distinction and champagne, and received the award from the Chancellor, Charles E. Young. Afterwards there was a grand reception and banquet at Chasen's attended by stars, network executives and advertising agencies.

Yorkshire had been desperate to break into the affluent American television market and still had not done so, yet on this grand occasion they failed to support me with even one handout. Lew Grade would have sent an army of salesmen and a ton of hard-sell literature. In a golden moment when the unknown Yorkshire Television was the target of every professional eye, I was absolutely alone. I spent most of the evening laboriously spelling my name to reporters who had never heard of me, or of Yorkshire TV.

After watching the programme everyone was most laudatory, once they knew who the hell I was. The Governor of California, Pat Brown, had just handed over to Ronald Reagan and become a lawyer. He asked if he could represent me in America. I agreed to everything, flew home—and was of course instantly forgotten.

Before I started filming again I had to face the ultimate penance of the Dumont Award; a lecture and interrogation before the UCLA Faculty of Journalism. This was the main centre of journalistic instruction in the land and, knowing how intense American students can be, how eager and ambitious, I was anxious not to let British television down before such a critical group.

I boned up on the wider implications of our programme and its background, the position of the United States within its Caribbean sphere of influence. I was apprehensive, but the massed undergraduates were an attentive and appreciative audience: alert reactions, laughter in the right places, endless notes. I completed my *tour d'horizon* amid unaccustomed applause, gratified by the impact.

The Dean made a few graceful remarks, and asked for questions. This was the testing moment. I braced myself for penetrating and informed demands, probably beyond my knowledge. The prize-winning film-maker at their mercy. After a long silence, a plump young women in the front row edged forward nervously. She had been absorbing my description of that Haitian life of terror with particular concentration.

'Mr Whicker,' she began, weightily, 'is it true that . . . you married an heiress?'

The whole Papa Doc experience had been full of fear and laughter, disaster and triumph—a black and sinister tragi-comedy.

*　　　　*　　　　*

In April 1971 President Duvalier died of natural causes—a rare achievement for any Haitian president. He was succeeded by his 19-year-old son, Baby Doc, who became the ninth Haitian since the 1804 Revolution to decide, like his father, to rule for life. That was his intention. He was later dismissed in a standard revolution and retired to live in some poverty in the South of France.

Papa Doc's fourteen-year rule had been marked by autocracy, corruption and reliance upon his private army of Tontons Macoutes to maintain power. He used both political murder and expulsion to suppress opponents. It was estimated that he killed 30,000 of his countrymen.

In 1986, after Baby Doc's exile, a mob stormed the Duvaliers' marble-tiled family vault to look for Papa Doc's body. The intention was to beat up his corpse to ensure that he could never rise again, even on Judgement Day. The mob was silenced and terrified to find the tomb empty.

They finally exhumed another grave, and beat up *that* body. Mobs are not selective. But was Papa Doc a zombie, out there working the fields?

3

TWO LHASA APSOS AND A COUPLE OF PANTECHNICONS

If ever there were a true 20th-century chameleon, it was Fanny Cradock. She invented reinvention. She had a number of names, and at various times had been an actress, journalist, romantic novelist, restaurant critic—apart from her own brilliant creation filling the Albert Hall as the original show-biz cook.

She was a television buccaneer years ahead of her time, and we met in her heyday, the time of cooking demonstrations before thousands where she would arrive on stage in white overalls and, just as the audience were sympathizing with her workaday life, strip off to reveal underneath a full-length crimson evening dress and diamonds—like Sean Connery unzipping his wetsuit. In the background Johnnie modestly revealed his white tie and tails.

There was nothing grey about Fanny. Everything was direct and startling: her opinions, her clothes, her generosity, her energy, her friendships and enmities, her impossible manners . . . This last trait was to be part of her undoing.

Fanny arrived in Jersey with Johnnie, two Lhasa Apsos and a couple of pantechnicons crammed with possessions. Also, strong opinions ready-made about everything and everyone.

They had left their home in Eire in fear after the murder of the British Ambassador in Dublin. She had grown afraid to turn on a kitchen light if the curtains were not drawn, and was scared of people lurking in the darkness around the house. It must have been a *very* serious scare for Fanny to admit to being frightened of anything. Alternatively it is just possible she had a noisy meeting, not with the IRA but with some inoffensive local shopkeeper who is still stunned by what hit him.

It is not easy to offend everyone in a small and tolerant island like Jersey, but Fanny managed it in a few short weeks. An innocent local photographer would be dismissed with a short sharp scream, a young waiter shyly proffering the Jersey Royals she was supposed to have cooked with her own skilful hands would receive a snarling, 'Take those away, we think they're *disgusting*' . . .

Her senior dog, which bit any hand that tried to feed it, sent our friend Ruby Bernstein dashing to the nearest hospital for a precautionary rabies injection, while wondering whether husband Albert—who had bravely sucked the tiny wound—should have similar treatment.

There was not much local sympathy, though I

34

did warn that the dog might suffer an attack of Rubies.

Fanny rarely enjoyed a smooth path. Writing a dreadful review of a long-established St Helier restaurant was hurtful. Jumping queues in the splendid fish market did not go down well, nor did complaining loudly at the butchers when waiting in the queue was the wife of the Housing Chairman. What started as little ripples of irritation became waves of discontent among island politicians: 'We've had one Norah Docker, we don't need another.'

It became obvious that Fanny did not much care for established restaurants, she liked to earn credit for discovering some hidden gem at the end of the jetty no one knew about. Fortunately this also extended to private cooks, as in Valerie's case entertaining was a new experience and each meal a hit-and-miss adventure. After that first dinner she was generous in her praise and managed to eat everything, only pausing as she left to offer a *bain-marie*. So far so good.

The Cradocks had been generous and hospitable when I was working in Fleet Street, so upon their arrival in Jersey I tried to ease their passage by arranging a lunch to introduce them to the great and good of the island. Fanny arrived dressed from head to toe in forest green, a veiled green bowler topping her orange make-up—a cross between Boadicea and Robin Hood. Her requested drink was predictably odd—Martini and sweet sparkling lemonade. This improbable mixture caused grinding of teeth and delay at the bar, and held up my distribution of conventional champagne.

After a short while she offered to help in the

kitchen. To discourage such good intentions we fed her first. Suddenly out of nowhere came a deafening crash . . . and there lay Fanny, flat out on the parquet like a green turtle. No movement, blood everywhere.

We hauled her upstairs and propped her up on a bed—hat and veil only slightly askew. A tentative search for injuries revealed nothing. Later it transpired she had gashed herself with her enormous rings. We went to warn Johnnie, who was sitting in his wheelchair by the dining-room fire, talking to admirers. We were worried the bloody incident might disturb him.

'Oh,' said Johnnie, noticeably undisturbed, 'she's done that again, has she?' He went on smoking his pipe. It was not my planned introduction to the Housing Committee.

They considered buying a pretty granite cottage a few hundred yards from us. We shivered a little, cautiously. In a way it was a shame. 'Given a choice,' I said, 'I'd rather keep a few parishes between us.'

This plan, like most of Fanny's good intentions, did not go well. A pity. There should always be room for the outrageous and the eccentric— though preferably *not* living next door. Eventually they settled in Guernsey, creating waves and mutterings of discontent. She was always high-handed and difficult, leaving chaos behind her and so much unpopularity that a local bookshop refused to stock her novels.

Causing a minor car crash at a crossroads, she blamed everyone else. Confronted by photographic evidence, she smiled dismissively: 'Just shows the camera can lie.'

We watched from the sidelines as her star dwindled. She shot herself in the foot on an Esther Rantzen programme, sneering at some poor housewife's attempt to cook a banquet. She was crucified by unkind editing—though what could you expect? In a few moments she was transformed from likeable monster to cruel bully, and her television career was over. She was probably the first fatal victim of a reality show.

We saw her a few months after Johnnie's death. Forlorn and broken, she was spending Christmas in a small Jersey hotel, doubtless one of those interesting little discoveries we had managed to avoid. She came to us for lunch and Valerie gave her a bulging Christmas stocking, full of delicious and caring goodies, but it hardly registered. The fire had gone out of her life.

Johnnie, hen-pecked and dominated all those years, had been her secret strength. Without him she let life go, and withered away. 'Nothing separates us, except rugby and the lavatory,' she had said, but now she was just a shell. Her old pugnacious fury had evaporated.

Our sacred monsters are different now: more beautiful, less genuine, more confident, less intelligent. They are created by PR and by management, not driven ambition. We know more about them but there are fewer layers to explore and no surprises. Everyone needs to test his courage against a Fanny Cradock, that furious pink stripe in a grey world.

CITY OF DREADFUL JOY

From a distance the contrast between life in California and life in Florida seems minimal—but close up these two golden states are a world apart. California, for all its self-conscious introspection, is a place to work; Florida is a place to retire, a sprawling mass of tidy housing and safe compounds, playgrounds for the like-minded old. Hard to imagine the far-out Wagners, Kurt and Kathy, a couple who had embraced every Seventies fad from Est to roller-skating, settling for life among golfers, bridge players and yoga.

Back in the Seventies Kurt would talk about an ageless society, a time when there would be no such thing as old age—as if the surgeon's knife could be the answer to all ills. These communities for the Sprightly Old do not quite match his prophecy, but their gated estates with gyms, pools and libraries are safe, warm and welcoming. In a country where youth is all, Florida provides an all-enveloping lifestyle for a group who would be invisible in many other states. Here, grey power has real power and the financial clout to back it up. Yes, bright sunlit winters *do* invigorate.

Aldous Huxley called Los Angeles the City of Dreadful Joy . . . However, he never found it so dreadful that he was tempted to return to the damp discomfort of Britain. For Anita Loos, actress and screenwriter who wrote *Gentlemen Prefer Blondes,* there was just no *there* . . . there.

For many journalists on the outside looking in, there was a sense of superiority, a thin-lipped disapproval of the Californian way of life that seems too easy, too relaxed, too open. Something rotten at the core, surely?

Old films show how our perception of America—particularly California—has changed. Now we all want a slice of that eternal sunshine, those excellent wines, the right to choose illusion before reality. In Beverly Hills, if it's not adequately beautiful, you change it. This could be a house—or a chin. That state of mind slid stealthily into our own world, so if the amount of happiness in your life is inadequate, go out and buy some more.

In LA, ageing without cosmetic surgery is now hardly an option. I suppose there may be women on those brilliant shopping avenues around Rodeo Drive who are indifferent to their wrinkles, but they have to be tourists, or foreigners.

Californian priorities used to be the pool, the second car—and after that, well, there's always something to remove, or tighten. Now it's unlikely that the pool and those cars would be on offer without the perfecting knife.

Before the Seventies, cosmetic surgery was a dark secret, a frivolous, guilty indulgence to be hidden from all but your closest friends. Names would be whispered and shared between those in the know, like that once-upon-a-time passing around of the numbers of surgeons willing to perform an abortion.

Many women would travel from the other side of the world for treatment by the famous Dr Pittanguy of Brazil, or an exotic Frenchman with a surgery in Tahiti. In London there was a man well known for experimental penis enlargement, an enthusiasm which for some reason never caught on . . .

In England where youth—that revolution discovered in the Sixties—had only just begun to take over, all this was still seen as the territory of the rich and spoiled, of actresses and their spin-offs. So when in the Sixties and Seventies I chose to look at the life and work of the Beverly Hills cosmetic surgeon Kurt Wagner, we inadvertently opened a window on a scene that was changing many lives.

I have filmed Kurt and his wife Kathy three times during these thirty-five years. They amused and irritated viewers in equal measure and drew mountains of mail from prospective patients. Outwardly content, living with the two daughters from his first marriage and an adopted son, they had all the trappings of Californian success—his Rolls, her Ferrari, their grateful patients, the perfect home in the Valley, a booming business in instant youth . . . what else *was* there?

Surgery aside, Kurt's self-centred arrogance and Kathy's breathy homilies on how to keep a husband happy were enough to keep a stoic British audience enthralled and appalled. With success came the usual California angst and the usual California panacea—therapy and infidelity, though not necessarily in that order.

I liked Kurt; he paraded his faults without concern—and Kathy was always instant joy. Piles of viewers' mail stimulated the protests, and the scoffing always came down to: 'Why can't they act their age?' It was the Palm Beach syndrome, stimulating the constant jealous rejoinder: they're too old to be having *that* much fun . . .

It wasn't always fun, not even with a top cosmetic surgeon in the family. Over the years there was disquieting news: Kurt's daughter had shot and killed herself on his bed with his gun. Kurt was arrested for receiving property stolen from the home of some renegade Saudi sheikh. He had been forced to sell his treasured collection of Toulouse-Lautrec posters. Their son had a drug habit. Kurt, bored with the beauty business, had invested their savings in Hollywood, of all places—and lost the lot. Chatty Kathy had taken to wearing exotic hats and wished to be known as Kathleen . . . yet to me she seemed, as always, uncomplicated and funny.

Filming *Journey of a Lifetime*, we found them living in Florida, miraculously still married after forty-one years. Kurt, in his fiftieth year as a surgeon, was back at work—this time in a sparkling glass building in Boca Raton full of the latest equipment for the war against ageing, into which he attempted to enlist me.

One particular machine was especially threatening. It could look into the future and show you what would happen to your skin should you choose not to take the expert's treatment and advice—a brilliant marketing device. One look and, aghast, you're calling your surgeon, any surgeon.

Kurt was heavier after another ten years, his face owing much to the latest techniques, the hair suspiciously thick and black. He had suffered two hip replacements and a brush with cancer. The old ebullient self-confidence was still there, but he was softer, kinder.

Kathy had not turned into prim Kathleen. Dressed in a leopard print turquoise top and three facelifts down the line, she was plump and giggly as ever. Furious with Kurt for losing all their money, she had forced him back to work and made it her business to be his living billboard. At clubs and parties she talked happily about her operations and encouraged friends to pay him a visit.

Leaving California had been a wrench for Kathy. She had thought of letting him go alone to start a new life in Florida but decided, upon reflection, that days spent breaking in a new man would be time-consuming, and possibly fruitless.

5

RELIEVING PATIENTS OF MANY POUNDS— ONE WAY OR THE OTHER

Anyone can be beautiful and loved: it's just a matter of applying something, taking a course, buying a pot, denying yourself—or being operated upon, slightly. Trying to keep up in the Face Race the average woman, when last counted, spends five years fourteen weeks and six days of her lifetime in front of a mirror. It certainly feels that way when you're waiting downstairs.

In view of all this I went to Texas at the birth of Spa Culture to observe the acolytes in The Greenhouse, the ultimate purpose-built fat farm or, if you prefer, health resort. This perfumed palace outside Arlington cost a million pounds to contrive and stands bathed in the soft glow of money, dedicated to the sale of dreams.

Women of a certain age (and some a little younger) were queuing to pay many hundreds of dollars a day for the possibility of rejuvenation. Some stayed months, refusing to give up. The ageing and wrinkled, the plump and the bored surrendered dollars and dignity in exchange for solace and repair, for the mirage of being lovelier and sexier—while outside in the harsh sunlight gardeners symbolically dyed parched Texas grass green.

In Britain, where we at least let grass decide its own colour, narcissism has also come to stay— observe the stately march of opulent health farms where the submissive can easily lose, along with avoirdupois, several hundred pounds a week. Only a couple of these country mansions were in operation when I filmed my first report in 1960; today scores of them are relieving patients of many pounds, one way or the other.

Even for *Panorama* it was hard to deal with the subject too seriously when the presenter was Richard Dimbleby, and not at all sylph-like. He came rolling up to me at the end of the programme, making predictably caustic comments about slimming. We also got a lot of irritable correspondence from enthusiasts after that, yet I have always held that for anyone with the money and the time such a regime can do nothing but good. It is like being lectured by Nanny and sent to bed without supper.

Establishments vary from earnest nature cure centres catering for those with little faith in

43

orthodox medicine, to antiseptic Victorian mansions where society matrons tussle with the years and Show Biz straightens its elbow.

For anyone not really sick, one of the cheerier hydros full of tubbies expensively repenting excess is a more agreeable retreat than those chintzy halls where arthritic old ladies knit by the fireside and silently disapprove of the merely weak-willed. The Surrey hydro where we filmed was populated by jolly carboholics resisting the temptation, alcoholics drying out and executives escaping the telephone: 'For a break my Chairman goes to the South of France and puts on a stone. I come here and lose one. He feels guilty; I feel great.' Both ways, it's expensive satisfaction.

One night during my recce I was watching television amid a subdued group in dressing gowns. The Saturday night play was just reaching its climax when a man in the statutory white Kildare coat strode in and switched off the set, in mid-sentence! I leapt up in outrage. 'Ten o'clock,' he said, reproachfully. 'Time for bed.' I was about to dash him to the floor when it came to me that this was exactly what we were all paying heavily for: a return to the secure days of Nanny knows best.

Once you have accepted such discipline there is a certain consolation in surrendering to father-figures who know what is good for you, having your days planned down to the last half-grapefruit. The carrot cocktail bar, where you sit and boast about the number of pounds you've lost, exudes a dauntless Blitz spirit and a communal sense of self-satisfaction at growing, if not lovelier, at least a little lighter each day.

Whatever the economic charts indicate, we are in the middle of one expansionist trend; at least 10 million men and 12 million women are overweight. We spend some £50 million a year on slimming foods which usually taste like crushed cardboard, exotically packaged lotions, complicated massage and exercise equipment, and pills—yet we all lose weight best by practising one magic exercise performed sitting down, though still difficult: you shake your head from side to side when proffered a plateful.

Insurance companies say that any man of 45 who is 25 lb above his proper weight has lowered his expectation of life by 20 per cent. Put in a more daunting way, he will go at 64 when he might have made 80. Repeat after me: No, thank you . . .

A sensible girl I took out in New York refused her apple pie *à la mode* with the boring chant, 'A moment on the lips, a lifetime on the hips'. She had a tidy diet which did away with tiresome calorie and carbohydrate counting: the Zero-Cal. She did not eat.

In California Elaine Johnson, a 35-year-old housewife, was 20 stone and so fat she could not cross her legs or sit without breaking the chair. She started her rigorous regime after getting wedged in a cafeteria doorway—a telling position from which to face facts.

At the same hospital Bert Goldner weighed in at 425 lb, or almost 4 cwt. He was so spherical he could not sit or lie without fainting from lack of oxygen, so had to sleep standing up or kneeling. During a nap he once toppled over and broke a leg.

In Beverly Hills I went to see that little round impresario Allan Carr, living in disco style behind

45

his guarded electric gates. He had made his fortune from *Saturday Night Fever* and *Grease,* and thought he had won a lifelong battle with avoirdupois after a major bypass operation ensured that all food would just slip through his stomach without registering. Many people undergoing that six-hour operation die of heart failure, so he did sincerely *want* to be slim.

During the next five years he lost 150 lb. Then, in the interests of staying alive, he had to have it all put back in old-fashioned order again, and immediately gained 75 lb. Allan Carr may be small and round and aggressive, but he is a man of decision: he had his jaw wired up so he could not eat.

'It also prohibits you from talking,' he told me, 'which is worse than not eating. I was very frustrated, as you can imagine, but you always carry little clippers around with you in case you choke or something, when you can snip the wires. So there I was sitting in the movie theatre watching Diana Ross in *The Wiz.*

'I knew it wasn't going to be good—I have these instincts about certain movies, so I didn't go to the première because I didn't want to lie to people, or hurt their feelings. I went on a Saturday. By the end of the first 45 minutes I disliked it so much, I was so nervous and agitated I just *had* to tell my friends what I thought about it.

'So I went to the men's room and took the clippers out and snipped my mouth open. I just couldn't stand not talking, at that moment. That's how I lost my mouth wiring. I'd had it on for ten days and I couldn't yell, I couldn't carry on, I couldn't talk on the phone very much. It was just terrible.'

One of the few remaining ways of drastic dieting open to him, I suggested, was sleep therapy, as practised in India, where it's a relief to stick to boiled eggs and a Coke.

'I've thought about it. You just go down to Rio for the Carnival, wear yourself out, and then sleep naturally for two or three weeks afterwards; but that's too slow, I haven't got the time to spare.'

I suggested he should travel to some of those places I had visited around the world where food was anything but enticing. He had done that, too: 'The best place is Egypt. It's like going on a scenic vacation and a diet at the same time. There's absolutely *nothing* you can eat in Egypt.'

Mixing with people with extreme weight problems makes one feel slim, instantly. Even *reading* diets offers a sense of quiet achievement; in a health farm it's positively therapeutic.

The form at our farm was a Sunday arrival with pseudo-medical test that evening: blood pressure, heartbeats, weight, and the old army how-do-you-feel routine. The usual treatment is a complete fast, by which they mean three oranges a day. Should you be determined to take on the world, reduce to three glasses of hot water a day, with a slice of lemon to take the taste away.

Mornings are filled with mild action: osteopathy, ultrasonic therapy, infra-red and radiant heat, saunas, steam and sitz baths, plus various combinations of sweat-inducing bakery: mud, wax, cabinet, peat and blanket baths. Best of all, massage and manipulation, which comes in all forms from distinctly painful to Wake up, Sir.

A health farm is rigorously asexual—all slap and

47

no tickle—but, as I always say, it's nice to be kneaded.

Looming ominously behind such agreeable time fillers, there are enemas and colonic irrigations. Nature-cure enthusiasts explain that in decoking the engine, waste poisons must all be swept away for a fresh, empty start—and that's the way they gotta go. This may or may not be medically sound, but it is not a thing I will willingly take lying down.

The various spin-off activities, or non-activities, seem more therapeutic: complete rest (or stultifying boredom); non-availability of demoralizing distraction, like pleasure; the spiritually uplifting and unusual sensation of being above temptation. I derived additional and permanent benefit by giving up smoking forty or fifty a day on the assumption that if I had to be mildly unhappy anyway I might as well be totally miserable. I have never restarted that horrible habit.

On a fast, with a dark brown mouth, cigarettes are as resistible as everything else. The whole system is so outraged, one further deprivation goes unnoticed. I commend this ploy to the addicted. I also—giant stride for one man—cleaned my car, a beneficial and constructive exercise which took care of two soporific afternoons.

Because of the pressure of television I have had no time for health farms for several years—so the car needed another visit even more than I did. Then the Metropole at Brighton launched the largest health hydro in Europe. I joined a cheery group drinking mimosas on a private Pullman from Victoria and submitted to the inaugural weekend of events and slimming treatments.

Without any struggle at all, I put on five pounds.

Nature cure, treated seriously, is not an expensive folly. Ignoring its unworldly cancer-cure fringe, the theory seems eminently reasonable: rest, restraint, simple food. Write off those who triumphantly smuggle scrummy-tuck into their bedrooms or creep off on afternoon dainty-tea crawls; their weighty problems are here to stay.

The ideal fortnight, down on the farm, is ten days' fast (during which you lose a stone) and four days' gentle return, via yoghurt, to salads and plain food. This puts four pounds back into that shrunken stomach. The more flab you take with you, the more you leave behind. Heavy drinkers and the very fat watch, fascinated, as it melts away and long-lost toes creep coyly into sight.

The benefit of the outrageous bill at the end of it all is that one may be stunned, upon release, into sensible eating—though most patients edge slowly up to the weight they took with them. Sterner souls change their life pattern—better and smaller people for ever.

All right—so I got the car cleaned.

6

RANDOLPH: AS RUDE TO AMBASSADORS AS HE WAS TO WAITERS

After the well-regimented, almost gentlemanly war I had known with the Eighth Army in Sicily and Italy, I saw at once that Korea was going to be something else: dirtier, more confusing, prisoners murdered, not a good place to be. There was no front line—every divisional HQ was in as much danger as its forward company.

As the US Army was due to rediscover in Vietnam, all an enemy soldier had to do to become a peaceful and invisible civilian was to hide his weapon, take off his jacket and stroll through our defences. I don't even want to write about their treatment of prisoners.

The war that we had just won with the capture of North Korea's capital, Pyongyang, was unwinding almost as soon as we'd finished their Hungarian caviare and champagne—a trifle sweet, but quite acceptable at that hour in the morning. We were sitting on the tatami after sleeping in ditches, so it felt like the Ritz, but we were not happy.

One of the early tragedies of any war is communication. At the front in the dying months of cable, a correspondent hands his story in to US Army Signals with blind faith and from then on it's up to them and the cable company, right through to Fleet Street.

Meanwhile the US Army apparently had too much on its plate to deal with us adequately. For a short period, all our messages were lost. This was the time for suicide or murder, knowing what we had risked to get those stories.

Along with most of the other foreign desks, ExTel despaired and gave up, telling me to make my way home to London. It was an escape clause: one such instruction was enough.

We were miserable enough anyway, with our missing copy which never left the battlefield. By then we were ready to catch any flight to anywhere that wasn't Korea. To ensure my final story got through, I had wangled a lift back to the Japanese mainland and handed the fragile news in to the Eastern Telegraph office in Kobe. At least I knew *that* story would be in London within a couple of hours.

In return the cable office handed me a mass of anguished messages from ExTel in London, warning me that few of my stories were getting through. The US Signals proved so chaotic that despite assurances from their PIO most copy had been mishandled, due possibly to incompetence or, more likely, unpleasant interference by the Chinese army. Correspondence had been lost for days—then sent full-rate.

Behind our backs, in a frozen Korea which we had left so triumphantly to return to Tokyo, the enemy had recaptured the capitals of Pyongyang and Seoul, and despite all this, or perhaps because of it, the Tokyo press corps continued to file and add to the piles of unsent messages, though it was no longer a big story. Both sides were closing down. The world was almost as weary of Korea as we were.

My recall was surrounded by Louis Heron of *The Times*, Tommy Thompson of the *Telegraph* and most of the fraught press corps. Front-line correspondents were moving back to their normal Far East stations, or going south to look at the increasingly threatening situation in French Indo-China which seemed favourite for the next upheaval.

In Tokyo, Gordon Walker, my friend with the *Christian Science Monitor* and an old Japan hand, drove me to Haneda Airport with Randolph Churchill and gave us our Japanese-style farewell

51

presentos. Then we boarded, flew towards Mount Fuji and home. It was a happy relief to surrender to the deep, deep comfort of a BOAC Argonaut.

Randolph, easily diverted by conviviality, had not been a spectacular success as a correspondent— though he wrote well enough when he wanted to. He had been flown out by the *Daily Telegraph* to replace poor Christopher Buckley, killed by a mine within an hour of reaching Korea. Unlike Randolph's father Winston, who had success as a correspondent in the South African war, he had little experience of the nuts-and-bolts legwork in the field of cabling and deadlines, nor, I suspected, was he much interested.

I had on occasion stepped in at the last moment when he was over-tired or emotional, to complete and file the *Daily Telegraph* piece for the unexploded Randolph. That may have been why I found this choleric character usually friendly.

He was also something of a celebrity, particularly among Americans. This was a new experience for me—'celebrity' was a different status which could prove a hindrance for other working press men who were not being asked for their autographs. Randolph, however, never objected to holding the stage.

'I can never win,' he told me. 'If I achieve anything they all say it's only because of Father, and when I do something badly they say, '*What* a tragedy for the old man.''

He was said to drink a couple of bottles of whisky a day, though I never ran into that. He had lost six attempts to enter Parliament, though he held an uncontested wartime seat in 1940–45. A biographer wrote, 'Aside from his heroically dismal

52

manners, gambling, arrogance, vicious temper, indiscretions and aggression, he was generous, patriotic, extravagant and amazingly courageous.' Michael Foot, a political opponent, said, 'I belong to the most exclusive club in London: "The Friends of Randolph Churchill".'

He and I planned to take a few days off during this return journey—from battle fatigue, you understand. First we went ashore in Hong Kong, where I bought an export Humber Hawk for eventual delivery at home, thus avoiding a waiting list of several years in the UK market, such were the idiocies of international financial controls.

Here we ran into the Churchill groupies again, chasing the son of the most famous man in the world. It was my first experience of autograph hunters and fans, for which we did not have much time. In Korea it had been a full-time job, and the target was merely to stay alive. Little did I know how life would change.

In Bangkok nobody knew who I was, of course, except that I was travelling with the noisy Englishman who was drinking. We were invited to dinner with the ambassador, which was not noisy at all, but I had the opportunity of observing Randolph on the social rampage. There's no doubt that, much as I liked him, after a few drinks he could become a responsibility. Excellent and amusing company, he was always in a state of suspended eruption. Other guests had to speak carefully in case he exploded. The nearest to a compliment you could get was to say that he was as rude to ambassadors as he was to waiters; he made no nice social distinction.

One evening Randolph and I filled in an hour of

happy irresponsibility pedicab-racing like gladiators through some deserted streets. It sounds most improbable today, when Bangkok shows us only fumes and endless jams.

This was the time when we called in the brilliant Noël Coward; his 'Mad dogs and Englishmen' started all the uncertainty. We could never be quite sure about these sharp lyrics: What did they do in Bangkok at 12 o'clock? Did they 'foam at the mouth and run' or possibly, as in Hong Kong, 'fire off a noonday gun'? I've *seen* that gun. We celebrated 'the inmate who's in late', and gave up. It was a relief to be singing about a war, instead of trying not to be killed by one . . .

Bangkok was a very suitable place to relax and watch some blue movies in a palatial House of Pleasure, appreciating the skill of a Thai cameraman which was delicate, even in gross situations.

I returned to London by way of New Delhi and Istanbul, and went on to cover the riots and revolution in Cairo and the Canal Zone. Randolph resumed editing his father's biography. It was business as usual.

*   *   *

My dictionary merely said, 'An oppressive hot southerly or south-easterly wind, blowing in Egypt in the spring'. That didn't sound too bad, yet it did have curious effects. For days the sun shone through low, hot sand clouds and the world was a hideous bright yellow, as though seen through a pair of cheap sunglasses. Gritty sand got into food, air and bed, tempers frayed, nerves stretched—it was the suicide season and it was not passing unnoticed for I had spent eight months in the Canal Zone, and noticed my occasional twitch and mutter.

'Shouldn't worry about it, old chap,' I told the shaving mirror one morning, after listening to some aimless chatter. 'A lot of people talk to themselves.'

As a foreign correspondent I was used to waking up in a different bed or a different country, but eight *months* in Egypt was a sentence devoutly to be avoided. We were all growing restless. 'I'd prescribe a short swan journey,' said James, soothingly. He was our conducting officer, appointed by the War Office to look after correspondents. 'Try Cyprus—it's our only escape hatch.' It seemed a wise weekend move.

A brisk transport captain offered me a berth on a troopship: 'You'll be in Famagusta in twenty-four hours. You can have three days of wine and women and be back by Monday.' He gave me what the army somewhat disdainfully called 'an indulgence passage'.

I threw a toothbrush into my typewriter, thanked James for the thought and sped up the Canal Road for Port Said, past the morning convoy of liners, oil tankers and merchantmen heading east. I was having an expeditionary pink gin in Navy House, enjoying the well-ordered peace of the RN, when a 10,000-ton American Liberty ship called, typically, *Joseph E. Brown* rammed the jetty with a fearful crash and nearly came upstairs.

Crunching through huge concrete slabs, the bows of the misguided *Joe* narrowly missed the stern of our cruiser *Cleopatra*. In keeping with traditional naval fun I urged my hosts to signal their Lords of the Admiralty: '*Cleopatra* raped!' They would not buy it. The captain gave a thin smile; I could tell he was thinking: 'Look, Whicker—*we* do the jokes.'

Inside the docks I hunted for the *Empire Sovereign*. 'That's it,' said a sentry. Nothing in sight except small harbour craft. 'There,' he said, pointing at the kind of boat which takes trippers from Richmond up to Kingston. 'No, no,' I said patiently, 'I'm looking for a troopship, ocean-going. Probably around 15,000 tons, promenade decks, restaurants, staterooms . . .' At that moment the words on the tiny stern came into focus: *Empire Sovereign*. 'Oh,' I said weakly, 'that's it, is it?'

Some troops were being handed lifebelts and ushered below decks and a few Cypriot workers were already being seasick. I was allocated a cabin the size of a medium wardrobe, with eight bunks. Eight! Two passengers were already established; the others, wiser, must have gone by air. Even with three, it was jammed.

When our little craft began to shudder we stumbled up on deck. A fusspot of a tug, only slightly smaller, nudged and chivvied us into mid-stream and we glided towards the Mediterranean, past the Simon Artz store, past the sky-high KLM sign and the broad beach, and those posh passengers travelling port-out-starboard-home.

Deck loudspeakers blared music and people waved from other ships. It was pure *Golden Eagle*. I felt we were bravely sailing to Margate, watching out for the Luftwaffe.

As we left the shelter of the harbour wall

something odd began to happen. The Med, as far as the eye could tell, was a millpond. Ignoring this, the *Empire Sovereign* forced herself through the water with a peculiar corkscrew motion—none of that straight up-and-down style ships have known and used for centuries. Passengers began to notice, and retreat below.

The troop commander, a pleasant CSM, came round with anti-seasick pills. 'I'm never sick,' I said, waving them away. We spiralled into another treacherous swoop. 'Well,' I said, clinging on, 'practically never.' He then delivered the clincher: 'It's 249 miles.'

We gathered silently in the miniature saloon: a sprinkling of army officers on swans of varying legitimacy, a middle-aged man with little brown hair and a lot of peroxide wig, a thin subaltern freshly married to a young army nurse. She, pale and about to be ill, disappeared morosely to spend her honeymoon night in the Ladies' Cabin (Gentlemen's, with chintz) and the groom mooched off down the companionway, kicking things.

A few of us attempted a meal, mostly at a very acute angle, and afterwards I rummaged through the ship's library. 'Real sailors' books,' mumbled an old Merchant Navy officer. He was wearing a beret, half-glasses, a woollen cardigan and looked like someone's granny. It turned out he meant 1928 throw-outs from seaside libraries, well-thumbed love stories about counts and heiresses. Certainly no meat strong enough to take mind off motion.

I bought a bottle of whisky for 15 shillings, and settled down with a paratroop officer who confessed he would have flown over but was frightened of *landing* in an aeroplane. Nobody would play poker, so we lurched off to our cabins, reminding each other it was only for twenty-four hours, after all.

I struggled up into a top bunk, and waited to be rocked asleep. During the night a gale blew up and it began to seem doubtful whether our gallant little ship could make it through the night. I was thrown to the deck three times, which is enough to wake anyone.

In the morning the weather was so bad we could not put into Famagusta, so while my Cypriot friends waited on the quayside my ship waited in a bay up the coast. We lurked there, a mile offshore and heaving, for four days. Nothing to read, nothing to do, drink all gone, madness coming fast.

On the fifth day the weather broke and I stumbled ashore, took a taxi to Nicosia and flew straight back to the Canal Zone and the khamsin. 'You look much calmer,' said James, when I reached the press dorm. 'Nothing like a holiday, eh?'

'No,' I said. 'Nothing like.'

7

NO ONE CARED ENOUGH

They were the generation of women who went into the '39 war and came out at the other end, unscathed but changed. Well-mannered, well-dressed, determined and resourceful, the Scarlett

O'Haras of the post-war years. Brought up expecting to live the opulent lives of their parents, they were aware such a world no longer existed, so, instead of clinging to the past, they reinvented themselves and became the bridge between Mrs Miniver and The Beatles.

Edana Romney was South African, creamy-skinned and red-haired. In the late 40s she starred in films, notably *Corridor of Mirrors*—remembered fondly by film aficionados for her endless close-ups. It was directed by a youthful Terence Young, who went on to tackle various James Bonds. She was married to John Woolf who, with his mischievous brother Jimmy, dominated much of the British film industry in the Fifties and Sixties—John a producer of significance, Jimmy a powerful agent and lover of Laurence Harvey.

Pictures of Edana show her in billowing evening dresses, waist cinched, a glittering show-business figure in a drab time of rationing and clothing coupons. All plain sailing until her marriage ended. Abruptly she did another Scarlett and began a new career in a new medium: she became BBC television's first agony aunt, with Edgar Lustgarten.

She moved into a stylish flat overlooking Hyde Park, rented Rose Cottage on the D'Avigdor Goldsmith estate near Tonbridge, and settled down with her elegant mother Min and Freddie the butler. It was an eccentric, stylish ménage that would survive some forty years of adventures on both sides of the Atlantic.

Chintzy Rose Cottage was transplanted lock, stock and steaming crumpets to San Ysidro Drive, a charming house in Beverly Hills, then to

59

Summitridge, once home of Corbina Wright, a notorious gossip columnist. They lived well, though by Hollywood standards frugally.

None of them had ever given a thought to driving a car—so here in California, where only the criminal or the eccentric actually *walk* anywhere, they lived in grand isolation. Connected to the world only by an overworked telephone, Edana settled down to a new career as a writer.

She had fallen in love with Richard Burton. Not Burton of the velvet voice and Elizabeth Taylor, but Burton the nineteenth-century adventurer and explorer. He translated the *Kama Sutra,* wrote about and patronized male brothels and polygamous Mormons and, risking death, coloured his skin for a forbidden visit to Mecca, Islam's most holy place.

For Edana it was almost an eighteenth-century life. She would stay in her boudoir most of the morning on the phone to friends, handing out advice and dreaming dreams of the dashing Burton. She wrote and rewrote her screenplay in a book annotated with ideas for location, strips of fabric for costumes and grand delusions: Sean Connery would play Burton, Richard Attenborough would direct. Someone once suggested that Tom Stoppard might rewrite the script. 'Tom *who?*' she said, grasping the project ever closer to her. She forgot that Hollywood promises have a shorter life than celluloid kisses.

Over the years, many years, Burton became an obsession. To finance her dream she visited the Sahara, courted the sheikhs of the Gulf and the Ivory Coast, mortgaged her home and her life and finally—lost everything.

60

The Manson murders terrified Hollywood but brushed lightly past Edana. Every high-profile actor expected to be shot or kidnapped any day, but Edana and I were invited to a party at the home of Joan Cohn, the movie mogul's widow and a major figure in Beverly Hills. It was an A-list party which would surely overcome the fears of the most macho film stars—indeed most of the great and the good in the film world were on parade.

We sat at the hostess's table, and the party was just getting going when, amidst a lot of shouting from the next room, the door burst open and in came a gang of Beverly Hills teens, led by our hostess's son. These rich kids were waving guns which looked like fakes to me, though the drugs certainly were not. I gathered from Joan's whispers that this kind of thing had happened before.

Hollywood is supposed to love a star—any star, even though they're always around in scruffy clothing at the neighbourhood supermarket or a favourite bar. At our table we had two popular detective heroes and a cowboy actor, but it seemed when guns were about they wanted a low profile. Thanks. All the stroppy rich kids were noisy, without being friendly. This was a situation where you needed a gun; a couple of shots into the ceiling would quieten things down. All the whispering guests at our table could think about was the Manson gang, and the fact that they shot to kill.

I explained to Edana that I now had one particular ambition, and that was to be somewhere else. I was planning to leave as soon as possible. If she came, I would distract the guns.

'I need some fresh air,' I said, quite loudly. One

of the flaky youngsters who had presumably been told to watch our table, was helping himself to our champagne and didn't seem interested in me. I filled our glasses and stood up, very slowly. That was the make-or-break moment of the evening. The kid still didn't seem to care about us, so I nudged Edana towards the French windows. Our guards were still busy shouting at each other. I opened one window. No shots rang out.

Everyone at our table seemed too petrified to move, so while our guard was in the next room finding out what was going to happen I opened the French window a crack. No reaction. I opened it wider and we slipped down some steps into the welcome darkness. We weren't followed or shot at, so headed towards some trees and distant street lights. Nobody joined us.

Within a few minutes we were out of that garden and walking through the shadows towards the Beverly Hills Hotel. I wanted to telephone the police, but was told it would not be a welcome move. It seems people preferred to keep hold-ups in the family.

When I checked I found they had not released our A-list table until the afternoon. They sat there all night, whispering and being frightened. No one was shot. I was thankful I was too busy to go out much and get to know the younger generation . . .

Meanwhile Edana's parties and entertaining continued in impecunious English country-house style. Not dinner—that would have been too expensive—but English tea on a Sunday afternoon: scones and thin cucumber sandwiches, one side brown bread, the other white, cakes, biscuits and endless tea. And the spoiled cast of

Hollywood came. Directors, actors, writers—she made it cosy and interesting, a sophisticated salon in an English country cottage in the Hollywood hills.

Peter Sellers was a near neighbour. He was renting a splendid house and was in good form, having completed *Being There* which he thought his best film ever. He explained why he wasn't very social with his British neighbours, like Edana Romney: 'They all get together and talk about Harrods.'

Sitting there on the mountain top looking down through the cypresses to Los Angeles, we laughed a lot while we filmed what sadly turned out to be his last interview. He was for once being natural and himself, not retreating behind funny voices. Usually when interviewed he became Bluebottle or Fred Kyte or an Indian doctor or any of those characters filed away in the recording machine between his ears which provided instant and precise playback.

He could not resist doing me, of course, the way everyone does. But then he unexpectedly stood behind my camera and ad-libbed a series of commercials about distant Britain. I was sitting there wondering what fee he would have required had he been commissioned.

In Hollywood everybody is a fan of somebody else. Roderick Mann, then show-business columnist for the *Los Angeles Times,* was sitting with Cary Grant when he whispered in awe, 'That's Duke Wayne over there!' Then one of the most famous comedians in the world, Peter Sellers was totally star-struck: 'I mean, to walk into James Stewart's office and see him sitting there, my mind

63

goes like *that*, you know. It's all I can do not to ask for his autograph.

'When I first came out to Hollywood they'd all seen *I'm All Right Jack* or something else of mine and my agent threw a party for me. Everyone was there. I was among people I'd only seen on the screen and I thought, Oh my God, and I figured on taking round my autograph book and asked my agent, "Would it be all right?" I didn't see these people very often. And he says, "Listen, you're going to see all of them for the rest of your life. You've no need to worry about him or him or him, that's the worst thing you can do."' Sadly, his agent was wrong.

Peter then had a reputation for being difficult. 'I always arrive on time and I know my lines and I'm a professional—but I can't stand the loonies, you see, I can't stand berks. This is the trouble.'

Not all Peter's colleagues were quite as enthusiastic about his professionalism; a friend worked with him during one of his unworldly periods when he drove the unit to distraction by continuously failing to turn up on the set. He would afterwards explain that his voices had told him not to work that day.

This happened so often and so expensively that finally the producer took him aside: 'Listen, Peter,' he said heavily, 'it's very strange that I've been hearing voices too, and you know what they told me? They told me if you're not in tomorrow and ready to go, both your legs'll get broken.' The voices were spot on.

Across the road lived the Harmsworth family. Pat 'Bubbles' Rothermere would arrive at Summitridge, her own bottle of champagne clasped to her bosom, and by her side a butler to open and pour. Parties were cast like films: the resident Brits, any new glamour, some writers, along with some new guys parachuted in for a few days, conscious of moving on quickly before the next new face arrived in town.

Sometimes there were small dinners for close friends. Occasionally there were dramas. Rona Barrett, columnist and radio star, arrived late—to be told by Freddie, as he flounced out, that her supper was in the oven, madam! Another time he rushed into the dining room in a panic as smoke poured through the serving door. Terence Young stripped off his Doug Hayward jacket to beat down the flames.

Once, lunching in the Beverly Hills Hotel Polo Lounge, I noticed something glistening on our banquette, and picked up a sliver of curved gold. 'Oh,' said Edana, 'that must be Grace Robbins's fingernail—she lost it last week.' She returned to her hamburger.

Three is never a restful number. Handsome Freddie was gay and alcoholic anyway, and paid only erratically—but everybody loved him. He looked splendid in his well-cut suits, and often acted as a dignified walker for Edana's unescorted single friends.

Edana did not drink but was addicted to sweets. She kept the drinks cupboard locked and the key hidden. There were many nights when, desperate for chocolate and fumbling her way to a secret stash, she found Freddie, nose glowing in the darkness, carefully topping up the whisky bottle with water. After spectacular rows there would be weeks when the two only spoke to each other through the gentle Min. 'Mrs Romney, please ask madam what time she requires dinner.' 'Mummy, tell Freddie we shall be dining at eight.'

Friends were loyal to Edana. John Woolf bought her a small house in the mountains behind Santa Barbara in Ronald Reagan country, and provided for her until the end.

She in turn was an enthusiastic and supportive friend. Whenever we arrived, a forest of plants and flowers would greet us. Later we learned that she had a deal with her florist. Whenever wealthy friends sent her extravagant arrangements she would send them back, ask for a credit and spoil closer friends as the occasion arose. This kept everybody happy, including the florist who could sell his flowers several times over.

She was always exceptionally kind to Valerie, particularly after discovering they were both Pisces—birthdays just two days apart. There was something magnetic about her, something rather wise. I could imagine strangers revealing secrets they'd be ashamed to tell a close friend. She loved and understood unconditionally, and was a brilliant listener. It was she who introduced me to Paul Getty, she who championed my film about Papa Doc which won the worldwide International Dumont Award for Documentary at UCLA, unheard of for a foreigner—let alone an Englishman!

We struggled to find ways to repay her generosity. I would send her cases of wine so that she could entertain in style, but knew that they would vanish in some deal. Once I sent her first-class tickets to London, only to discover she had instantly cashed them in. It was not easy to help her without appearing to know that she needed help.

There was a man in her life. Good-looking and reserved, he seemed to spend a great deal of time in Guam. We were assured he had something to do with the CIA but it may have been more sinister, or more prosaic. He was quite generous, and gave Edana huge slabs of jewellery. 'I wish I'd got into this a bit earlier,' she murmured, surprisingly unworldly.

She had taste and ingenuity. She could decorate lavishly—or on a shoestring. I remember her telling one friend: 'I will make your home a jewel box in which you can shine.'

In London she helped me furnish my apartment in Cumberland Terrace, Regent's Park. One lunchtime, while choosing carpet in Heal's, she went to the loo and found herself locked in. I, meanwhile, had found newspapers and Bernard Levin, who was also moving into a new home. We failed to notice her absence. Hours passed before she was released, speechless. Not unreasonably, she was very angry indeed—outraged at not being missed.

Trying every avenue to finance the Burton film, she became friends with Sheikha, a Gulf wife who still lived the closeted life of the harem. Edana relaxed into it and loved it. It was warm and luxurious, with much lounging about in dressing-gowns, attended by endless servants in grand palaces and country houses. All went well until the day the servants were off and Edana, who rarely cooked, volunteered expansively to prepare dinner.

After muffled phone calls to Min, she decided

that a joint of lamb would be the smart choice. Armed with instructions, she strode confidently into the kitchen to find a whole sheep, fleece intact, lying on the table and awaiting dissection. In floods of tears, she made desperate calls to Robert Carrier, who saved the day.

Many directors nibbled at the Burton idea, including Richard Attenborough, looking to follow his *Gandhi,* but no one would take the project with Edana at the helm, and she would not budge. She was in love with her subject. Burton's fiancée had been heard to say, 'If I can't be him, I shall marry him.' Edana had also devoured his spirit, and refused to share him with anyone. She would brook no changes in scene or dialogue, and year by year, promise by broken promise, she lost her dream, and then her home.

She moved first into the guest villa of her friend, the owner of the Beverly Hills Hotel. We were shown proudly around the main house. A dressing-table drawer revealed hundreds of lipsticks, each neatly upended and numbered. An armchair had a cord across its cushion, as in a museum, to be looked at but not sullied by some unknown bottom.

This luxury life ended abruptly. A whispered and tactless phone call overheard by her hostess, a golden gate slammed forever. For years there was always some miraculous safety net. This time, the Princess of Hyderabad, a beautiful lonely lady who invited Edana to look after her San Ysidro home. Later, in the house which John Woolf had built her across the valley, she and Freddie glided happily through a complete facelift, a benign brain tumour and a hip replacement until, at 93, Freddie died and, in effect, Edana died with him.

She took to her bed and never left. She was moved from one clinic to another as she dwindled, like some parcel with insufficient stamps, and we lost her. Her friends were somewhere else—in London or South Africa, Jersey or Beverly Hills. This extraordinary lady vanished. No one cared enough.

8

STILL NO DEAL WITH THE DEVIL

The Tokyo Chapter of the Baker Street Irregulars was formed a few years after the '39 war—we were on to *another* war, by then: the Korean, which was much nastier. Some years later my friend Richard Hughes (*Sunday Times* and *Economist*) presided over a small but distinguished group who—after a hearty eleven-course Japanese banquet accompanied by an admirable Imperial Nada *sake*—decided that Sherlock Holmes's first meeting with Dr Watson in Piccadilly Circus should be honoured by a plaque. Holmes, who wanted to rent some of his Baker Street rooms, greeted Dr Watson with a telling: 'You have been to Afghanistan, I perceive?'

The plaque was unveiled at a televised ceremony commemorating the historic meeting early in 1881 at the original Criterion Long Bar. Then on the morning of Derby Day 1956, after its years on the wall outside the Criterion, two young men stole it. Their identity has never been discovered. A dastardly crime, indeed.

The crime was partially rectified when, seven years later, the plaque was surrendered. A stranger claimed that he had 'found' it in a house just purchased in Wimbledon. To Sherlock Holmes it would doubtless have been a piffling one-pipe mystery. The Irregulars did not find it so elementary.

Richard Hughes, the Rabelaisian Australian correspondent, had been widowed and was managing the Tokyo Press Club in the Shinbun Alley when we met. There were side benefits, even forty years ago: $80 a week, plus free board and half-price drinks. This was considered a good deal, though not good enough to halt the move down to Hong Kong, as Japanese domestic prices climbed out of sight.

Dick was large and Pickwickian—though financially closer to Micawber. He called our ultra-casual club 'Alcoholics Synonymous'. When in Hong Kong, a dozen or more of us would meet upstairs at Jimmy's Kitchen in Central, or in the Grill Room at the Hilton where a bust of Dick presided over his usual table. Those found worthy were appointed 'Hatmen', because if a message should arrive warning that any one of us was in trouble, the reaction would be *instant:* 'Gimme me hat.' This imperative recalled Dick's Australian origin. (I fear the call to arms may be too late for some of us . . .)

War correspondents go through a lot of life and death together, and the Korean War was dangerous and exciting enough. In Fleet Street I might run into a friend who shared my jeep for a few treacherous days before Pyongyang—and we'd pick up the conversation mid-sentence. Such a close relationship was fired in danger, though rarely survived a home posting.

After the war, in true Hatman tradition, Dick dropped everything and flew to London to say kind things on my *This Is Your Life* programme, recalling the moment I was reported—with some exaggeration—shot down and killed on the Korean front.

The first time I saw Dick after my brush with the North Korean artillery was when I entered the Radio Tokyo press centre on my way back from Korea, to learn that I was a ghost. 'My God,' he whispered, 'you're *dead.*' There's a limited number of replies to that.

To support this disturbing news he showed me the story he had just filed detailing the whole unhappy incident, supported by two (very short) pieces on the front pages of the *Daily Mail.* They recorded the death in action of yet another Allied correspondent, followed by a Reuter's obit. That seemed to settle the matter. I was a statistic—and so young.

In fact the Royal Artillery in Korea had that morning put up two Piper Cubs as aerial observation posts over the front line. On my way back to Kimpo and on to Tokyo, I was offered a hot seat in a Piper Cub, and was too cowardly to refuse. So, teeth clenched, I was spotting targets in the plane that was *not* shot down.

Some years later, when I was surprised by Eamonn Andrews and various friends and colleagues, Dick came on stage to explain my fatal crash, quite easily: 'The front page story in the *Daily Mail* said he'd been lost in action, and we presumed the press can't be wrong. It gave us an admirable excuse to sink a few drinks and to toast one of our friends—a great reporter and great interviewer who proved once again what our mutual friend Ian Fleming said, "You're only as good as your friends."'

I did not instantly recognize myself, until Dick was followed on stage by Huw Wheldon, then the BBC's Controller of Television. He continued the flattery—sort of—by telling Eamonn, 'He's a magnificent journalist and a first-rate television reporter, but the really interesting thing about Alan is that he looks like an inquisitor, he looks stern, but in fact he's got a heart of gold. He's kind and benevolent—people actually *like* him.

'But those terrible glasses, that accusatory countenance and mordant turn of phrase, that grated voice that says, "Don't you *dare* lie to me!" Yet he is in fact good-humoured and lets people speak for themselves. He has no victims, only friends—everybody loves him.'

We lovable Hatmen met when possible in an upstairs room at Jimmy's in Central Hong Kong, a regular booking under the club's title: Alcoholics Synonymous.

Knowing the fearful price of communication even in those days, I let the ExTel know of my good luck in cablese: *Uninjured, Unkilled, Onpressing.* Transmission then cost 1/1½d a word so it seemed—to me at least—a well-spent 40 old pence that covered my situation adequately.

When the war ended most Far Eastern bureaux moved from Tokyo down to Hong Kong, where you could live more economically. The Press Club was then a fine villa on Mid-Levels which had been the setting for the William Holden film *Love is a Many-splendored Thing,* based on a novel by Han Suyin about her love affair with the *Times* man Ian Morrison, an early fatality in Korea.

Dick was larger than life, and funny until his death. At his memorial service at St Bride's, Fleet Street, I sat with Denis Hamilton who was then running the *Sunday Times.* I told him, gently, that after a lifetime of bylines and journalistic significance, Dick was facing retirement strapped for cash. Denis arranged a substantial ex-gratia payment to his family.

Dick's death left a void that clouds my every return to the Far East. On the night of that mournful Handover of the colony to the Chinese, I could sense Dick's disapproving shade castigating 'the running dogs'.

The massive HK-Hilton has now been developed out of existence—and since Dick's gone, *what* has happened to the bust presiding over his table in the Hilton Grill? Could he be, as the Chinese call us, a white ghost?

Even today when I think of that endearing man who left us in '84, I smile. He had been immortalized by John le Carré as Old Craw in *The Honourable Schoolboy.* 'Some people, once met, simply elbow their way into a novel and sit there till the writer finds them a place. Dick is one,' said the author. 'I'm only sorry I could not obey these urgent exaltations to libel him to the hilt. My cruellest effort could not prevail against the affectionate nature of the original.' Dick was also Dikko Henderson with James Bond in Ian Fleming's *You Only Live Twice,* and Yer Grace to admiring friends.

A warfront friend of mine, Tommy Thomson of the *Daily Telegraph*, came out to replace one of the many casualties of the Korean War. In his book *Cry Korea*, Tommy's dedication saluted 'Those correspondents whose friendship and fortitude lightened the darkness of the worst of these days, and whose courage and integrity are not the least hope of mankind'.

I was one of the first correspondents *en route* for the front to check into the Commonwealth officers' hotel in Tokyo, the Marunouchi. In those days the Japanese were a very small race indeed, and the little wood-lined bedroom was a tiny third-class cabin. The bed was a child's bunk and I had to bow low to the washbasin. The Japanese have grown up since 1951.

The first person I saw in the hotel bar that evening was Christopher Buckley, a wartime friend from the battlefields of Africa, Sicily and Italy. Senior correspondent with the *Daily Telegraph,* tall, stooping and professorial, he was in line for the Chair of the History of War at Oxford. He had made his name with the Eighth Army's trio of war correspondents in the western desert with Alan Moorehead (*Daily Express*) and Alex Clifford (*Daily Mail*).

He had just married for the first time relatively late in life, and was understandably enamoured of his new wife. When we went in to dinner I was touched to see them holding hands under the table.

Christopher and I had just returned from fighting a long war, and were now horrified to find ourselves on our way back to another one, so we talked earnestly about Destiny and the ever-present prospect that some cataclysm might destroy all that made life worth living. We both found it strange to be back in uniform again so soon, as though destined to soldier the years away while the world lurched from war to war.

After his recent years of war, Christopher was fatalistic: 'I wish I could do a deal with the devil,' he reflected, in an echo of that other Christopher—*Dr Faustus*—as we sat in the chill air conditioning eating hearty Australian rations made delicate by Japanese chefs. 'If I could be guaranteed ten years without a war, ten years of uninterrupted happiness so that my wife and I could go back to Italy and buy a villa and settle down to write in peace . . . then I'd willingly give up what was left of my life. The devil could take my soul and the rest of me.'

Being young and eager and believing there were answers to all questions, I protested against such a despairing view of the future. He should not be ready to accept such a rotten deal. 'I'm shooting for 80,' I said, thinking of a number (which, it would seem, I should have made higher). When it came to collecting, the devil may have come out too well.

They were both quietly adamant that a sure guarantee of ten years of undisturbed tranquillity would be an acceptable bargain, so I gave up.

Next morning Christopher said goodbye to his wife, who was to wait for him in Tokyo, and we boarded a transport C54 and flew to Korea, at the start of a new adventure. At the Taegu airstrip we separated to set out upon our first war story. I hitched a lift with some officers of the US First Cavalry Division I had just met, while Christopher

75

joined the United Nations jeep of a friend, an Indian Army colonel, Unni Nayar, bound for another area.

An hour later they hit a mine. Christopher was killed instantly. Had he done that deal with the devil he and his wife would have been exactly ten years in credit, minus one day.

He was buried near the *Times* man Ian Morrison on a hillside above Taegu. It was going to be a horrible war.

9

IN AMERICA'S SMARTEST SOCIAL RESORT ONLY THE LONELINESS GETS WORSE

Mrs Pamela Symes ran Gucci's jewellery department in their elegant store on Worth Avenue, Palm Beach, dizzier than which you cannot get. She had a crystal-cut English accent and dangling horned-rims and was extremely thin and elegant. You'd think it might be too much for Gucci's American followers, but it seemed to appeal.

She had lived alone for twenty years with Sinatra, a Siamese cat—'ole blue eyes'—as a best friend. She had trouble remembering her own phone number, so presumably did not receive too many calls, though she operated within the heartland of the savage society world of ultra-rich and heavily bejewelled matrons.

She was gradually slipping into relative poverty amid the elegant army of widows in the cruel social

76

world of Palm Beach. Mrs Symes was quite matter-of-fact about her circumstances and not in the least sorry for herself as she faced another solitary holiday at the heart of the resort's frenetic social whirl, which she could watch, but not join.

In America's smartest and most social resort, only the loneliness gets worse as you grow older: 'It's the sharing that's lost,' she told me. 'My husband died twenty years ago—but I still want him to see something I've seen, still turn round to share a joke with him.'

Next day, talking to Pam while she crisply controlled her counters, we managed to slip her out for a coffee while the staff fawned over Dr Aldo Gucci, the founder and creator of the dazzle surrounding us, who was on a royal visit.

I asked Pam whether she might ever retreat to live again in England. 'Oh heavens, no. I couldn't stand it. The weather kills me. You work like a slave—which is fine, because I work like a slave here—and you look forward to the three weeks when you can run away to somewhere warm. When I left England I was freezing to death and I vowed I would never again *pay* to keep myself warm, and I haven't. I've been away too long. I've not actually lived in England since 1954.

'The first time I went back I was appalled because it depressed me so much. All the friends I had in those days have scattered over everywhere. I've lost touch with them, and London can be an incredibly lonely place to live in. Furthermore I doubt very much whether I could afford to live there as I live here. I'm a working woman but I live remarkably comfortably. I have a very pleasant apartment, run a car, go away on holiday. If I was doing in London what I do here, I think I'd have to live in the outer wilds of God knows where—some slum in Ealing—and perhaps give myself a treat once a month by going up to town for a meal.'

Mrs Symes denied that in Palm Beach women had to be rich. 'They just have to be very *monied,*' she said, splitting a hair. 'To see a young woman of fashion in the season in Palm Beach is a miracle. They're mainly widows. It's like the South of France with, what, six women to every man? They're all 60-plus, you know, and all the men floating around, unless they happen to be husbands, are young men who escort the ladies. To all intents and purposes: gigolos. The women who come down here have followed the season from place to place. They all live the same sort of life: bridge parties and dinner parties and charity affairs.

'There are still people down here, because of the age group, who think a dinner party *has* to be man, woman, man, woman—and there just aren't the men. So they acquire all these peripheral escorts who are only too delighted to eat out. If you wear pants and you're alone you can eat out somewhere every night of your life, as a guest. Being English helps. As soon as you open your mouth—but it isn't so much that you're English, it's that you're *different.*'

I wondered what she did at this time of intense loneliness for every solitary person.

'Various people say, "Oh do come and join us," but I don't really like to because I make a series of phone calls to friends and people all over the world on Christmas Day and then I have my darling little Fortnum & Mason Christmas pud with brandy sauce. Another thing that's very important to me—I go home and undress, climb into a robe and don't dress again until it's time to go to work the day after.

'Usually when I finish my day's work I totter off home, have a glass of milk and talk to Sinatra. There's an excellent library in Palm Beach and I love old movies, so I belong to cable TV's old movie channel, which is delightful.'

I wondered whether there was anything she missed from London, at Christmastime.

'Yes, the theatre. There's nothing like the London theatre, nothing, and I must admit that occasionally I start thinking about wonderful things like Scottish salmon and pork pies and bangers and mash and Young's potted shrimps with brown bread and butter . . .'

Could she see herself ending her days here in the sun, with Sinatra?

'God forbid—I don't think I'll be able to end my days in Palm Beach because I'll not be able to afford it. Comes the moment when I can't work any more, then I really don't have enough money to live on. I'll look for somewhere warm. I shall have whatever it is the Americans dish out because I've been here long enough, but it isn't all that much and Palm Beach is one of the more expensive places in the States. I honestly don't know what I shall do.

'I avoid the issue, I really do, but I smoke heavily. Hopefully I won't live too long. I'm serious, because youcan't afford to be ill here and you certainly can't afford to *die* here. In addition to which, as you get older, you get lonelier.

'I have a system. My husband has been dead for

twenty years and I haven't found anybody that I particularly think is thrilling and neither have they found me, let's be truthful about it, so I think I face a rather miserable and lonely old age. All my contemporaries have popped off so I'm hoping I shall pop off also. I really would very much like it if I could pop off before it gets to the moment when I'm too ancient to work. That would suit me very well.'

When Mrs Symes left Gucci a few years later she moved to a retirement home, but soon after—as this dauntless woman would surely say—she got her wish and duly popped off as she hoped, independent, fearless and correct as ever.

10

YOU DIDN'T LOOK LIKE THAT IN *HELLO!*

In the years before the British colony was handed back to the Chinese government, it was said that no occidental marriage lasted more than a few months after the husband accepted a posting to Hong Kong, such was the charm and quality of available secretaries and salesgirls, and their desperation to get a foreign passport. Western men were enchanted by the delicate subservience of Asian women—they seldom noticed the rock-hard, clear-eyed ambition behind those soft voices.

On a recce for our BBC series we had spent the day in the notorious Walled City, that foul and lawless no man's land in Kowloon. Bulldozed from memory some years before the Handover to

China, this dank, heaving labyrinth of alleys and open sewers was home to Triads, giant rats, heroin addicts and criminals. Ragged children squatted in the dirt, cats were kept in cages to protect them from predatory vermin, dim sum was prepared in squalid little food factories, the plates washed in muddy puddles. It was the underside of Hong Kong's addiction to making money and far from the shiny new buildings and shopping centres that overwhelm tourists.

Hours later, as though we had stepped through the looking-glass, we were in a different world. A grand dinner party had been arranged to greet us at the newest and glossiest hotel. In a tall glass atrium jutting over the harbour, the lights of Hong Kong island dazzled across the water. Our hostess had invited a selection of faces from the pages of the Hong Kong *Tatler* to look at us—or perhaps for us to look at them.

The table was set with a Cartier dinner service; bread rolls were stamped with the double C logo. After a day wading through squalor, the dinner was a difficult setting to live up to. A disappointed colonial wife stared disapprovingly at Valerie, shaking her head, and issuing her judgement: 'You didn't look like that in *Hello!*' That was true.

Around the table the women were impeccably dressed, most in uniform: little gold-buttoned Chanel jackets neatly skimming their tiny bodies, the men darkly suited and rather solemn. Gerald Godfrey, seated beside Valerie, was a smooth, amusing Englishman fluent in seven oriental languages and, having spent most of his life in Asia, more Chinese than European. His shoes were highly polished, his clothes just slightly wrong. He had the louche air of someone who didn't quite fit in—not uncommon in places like Monte Carlo or Palm Beach, where reinvention is a part of life.

Quite suddenly he stopped talking and gazed out across the water. Sailing past the vast window of our splendid dining room was a tiny junk, its tattered white sails flapping in the night wind, a relic from another age. 'Look at that,' he said. 'You'll never see it again.' It had touched something within an old China hand.

Opposite us sat Cecily, his beautiful Korean wife, unsmiling and angry. Through the severity of her expression it was impossible to tell her age. With polished black bob and camellia-white skin she might have been 30—or 50. We left that dinner bemused by this ill-matched couple, never imagining that we would become friends.

Gerald had started his working life in Thailand, later moving to Hong Kong and into partnership, professionally and personally, with the legendary Eurasian art dealer, Charlotte Horstman. By the time he met his future wife he was living a playboy life in one of the last ancient houses in the colony, the former country residence of the Bishop of Hong Kong.

Cecily, born in Korea but educated in the United States, was a dress designer. She married young, had a daughter, and divorced. On her first date with Gerald he took her to a seafood restaurant where they ate soft-shell crab. He relished his carefully, and tidily stowed each bony leg into its empty shell. She scattered her remains over plate and table.

He looked across and thought: *What* a mess. She

thought: Must be gay. After this inauspicious beginning, and with considerable hesitation on both sides, they married.

Their house, set in two acres of some of the world's most expensive real estate, was a little thatched jewel. They grew their own vegetables, kept cats and fighting cocks and were looked after by a brigade of Filipinos. Apart from the odd snake living under the eaves, everything was impeccable. When they entertained, vintages from the year of the guest's birth would miraculously appear—or should that prove to be a bad year, the year of conception would substitute. Huge ladles of caviare were served in bowls shaped like lily-pads and the garden lit with flaming torches. It was a fairytale setting, a stage set for customers and friends to enter for a few hours, a world where everything appeared perfect.

With the Godfreys, nothing was ever left to chance. They would take their own wine in a hand-stitched leather carrier to the grandest of restaurants. Always there would be an element of theatre: a snake might be brought in, its stomach slit open, gall bladder removed and guests encouraged to drink the bitter green bile—a prized aphrodisiac, though usually a step too far for the white ghosts, their squeamish *gweilo* guests.

Little by little it became evident that Cecily, though some twenty years younger than her husband, was the stronger of the pair. He was the risk-taker, the gambler, the collector and the dreamer. She was the astute perfectionist and brilliant saleswoman. In their go-down, the huge underground treasure house beneath their showroom at Ocean Terminal, they employed a team of immaculately dressed salesgirls who were informed by their beady-eyed boss that if she ever caught them flirting with a prospective buyer they'd be sacked on the spot: 'The girl flirts with the husband, the wife sees . . . I lose a customer.' There were no second chances.

Gerald once explained the Korean philosophy as: You won't do what I want so I am throwing myself out of the window—*then* you'll be sorry. At the Foreign Correspondents' Club the old hands would sigh over demonstrations in Seoul, saying that on principle journalists always supported student rebellion . . . but they made an exception in the case of the unlovable Koreans.

As a cool perfectionist Cecily was admired, though not much loved. At a London dinner party another art dealer was staggered when he heard someone claim to be a friend of Mrs Godfrey. 'I've never ever heard anyone say *that* before,' he exclaimed, shocked. This seemed a little unfair. She had great passions and enthusiasms that came in short bursts, sometimes for people, more often for horses or swimming or ballroom dancing—and it became evident that she felt like a butterfly beating its wings against a golden cage.

Cecily had vivid memories of a childhood lived through the Korean War, of hunger and hardship, of her mother complaining to an officer about a stolen radio and the young suspect instantly shot dead in front of them.

She seldom mentioned her father, except to say that he had his own life; he was not expected to come home at night, and that was accepted. She said, 'We don't have the Western concept of love, we do not believe in romance—marriage is about

84

status and money.' Most important in her life was 'face'—how she was perceived and how she treated other people, the idea being never to inflict embarrassment or humiliation or to suffer it in return. Not an easy path to tread for one so intransigent. A society woman, director of a famous auction house, was unwise enough to suggest that Cecily might be lesbian. 'Ring up Lord C, I want her sacked,' was the reaction. Not too many worries about face in that instance . . .

She had been to Korea for some discreet cosmetic surgery—'Always Korean doctors, far more dextrous. See how they use their silver chopsticks—far more difficult than Chinese ivory, or wood.'

Bored and irritated within her marriage, she was ready for an adventure. Choosing a younger man, she planned her lunchtime assignation in a hotel close to her office, to save time. Warned that this was not a brilliant idea, she said not to worry—her secretary had booked the room. 'I'll give her an old Chanel handbag, and she'll shut up,' she said, full of confidence. Days later she reported she would not be repeating the experiment. The man's performance was not up to scratch. Gerald had been far more virile when he was that age and, worse still, as her secretary had made the reservation, Cecily did not get a discount.

After this disappointing experiment she surrendered to the latest Hong Kong craze: ballroom dancing. With her usual determination she soon became the star of her class. One day, leaving her lesson and for some reason without car or driver, she was caught in a downpour. 'I was in my new skirt and my new shoes and there were thirty people waiting for taxis. I was getting wetter and wetter, so I pulled a $50 note from my wallet and waved it until a taxi stopped. I got into his horrible car with water pouring through a hole in the roof, my feet in a puddle—and I thought: Better to stay married!'

They came to stay with us in Jersey, an unusual couple with Vuitton luggage and huge tins of caviare. Not the usual visitor profile of grey-suited businessmen or cheery beach gear. They were instantly stopped at Customs: an Eastern beauty and a quiet blue suit. Chinese? Middle Eastern? Naples? Immigration were baffled. The capo di tutti capi? Hold it, George—I think we've got a big one . . .

Then they mentioned they were coming to stay with us—and were instantly ushered on their way to our house, with smiles.

I gained *enormous* face.

As 1997 and Hong Kong's Handover to the Chinese approached, we sensed their preparation to withdraw. All around them people who, years earlier, had fled the Communist mainland were discovering new pride in their Chinese roots. For the Godfreys, ever pragmatic, it was important to be close to the new masters. There were no more flamboyant dinners in fashionable restaurants for *gweilos*. It was best not to be seen with us. White ghosts belonged to the past, not the future.

Listening to a radio phone-in days before the Handover ceremony we heard a succession of tearful voices ringing to thank the Governor, Chris Patten, for trying to bring more democracy to the colony. Cecily insisted that he was despised, that this was the Chinese way—send him away with a smile so that he doesn't lose face. She was jubilant that, at the actual rain-swept ceremony, Gerald had been seated in Row 2, poor Lady Thatcher in Row 7.

At the end of our stay we had one last dinner at a discreet restaurant, a joyless meal, Cecily resentfully driving us back to our hotel in the drizzle. It was clear that our friendship was over. We were much saddened—with or without face.

Years passed. Flying from Australia or Bali we would spend a few days in the former colony. At times it felt as though the balloon had burst, that all the brash vibrancy and sparkle had left the island and gone to Shanghai, that Hong Kong would become a forgotten backwater, a little colonial hiccup best forgotten. Confidence returned, different faces looked out from glossy pages or sat in the Mandarin Grill, but little else had changed. However, there was no sign of the Godfreys—no one saw them or spoke of them. They had disappeared. An impeccable lifestyle had vaporized.

This year, filming *Journey of a Lifetime,* we returned once again to our favourite place. Again we asked after our old friends. There were embarrassed pauses. 'She is dead, she killed herself.' Unhappiness, disappointment, depression —another woman? There were hurried explanations, none ringing quite true. No one wanted to tell us what had happened, even if they knew. It was as though talking about Cecily would invite bad luck. Like characters in a Scott Fitzgerald novel, all trace of the Godfreys and their world had vanished. They are missed.

11

IN MEXICO DEATH KNOCKS MORE OFTEN AND MUST MORE FREQUENTLY BE ADMITTED

Mexico seemed like a blow in the face. I was stunned by its beauty and squalor and excitement. From the first day of filming we were nervous and stimulated. No one could be indifferent to this dramatic and passionate land, tormented and violent, hateful and lovely. Some courteous Mexicans are chic worldlings, others move in the dark of superstition.

The red of blood and the black of death have always stained a nation where many face a future that does not exist, and a distant past they dare not remember.

Today they are part of one of the world's biggest population explosions, for Latin America can lead Africa and even Asia in its birth rate. In the thirty-five years between my visits, the population grew from 35 million to 98 million. Mexicans, they say, are very good at making babies—it's one of the demands of *machismo*.

The pleasures of the poor must necessarily be simple. The peon who works all day for a plate of tortillas and beans has one compensation: his wife. As both now live a little longer and more children survive, the benefits of progress are spread thin.

Mexico City is ringed by its belts of misery. Within sight of opulent high-rises, millions of homeless have 'parachuted' on to vacant land. The penniless and usually illiterate peasant, driven from the land by a government policy of giving way to strong industrial unions by keeping agricultural prices artificially low, comes to Mexico City with his family to hunt for work, and sinks despairingly to live in some *favela*.

Such is the human spirit that sometimes pride and amiability remain. At least the benevolent Mexican sun softens the harsh outline of existence. It could be said that in some ways Mexicans are more free than at any time since the days of their magnificent ancestors, the Mayans, who knew zero 1,500 years before Europe discovered decimals.

Once the doorways of the capital were jammed every night by freezing bundles of newspapers that were homeless boys. Much of the population had no shoes, and for men the only protection against summer rains and winter nights was *pulque*—a spirit made from cactus. For women, it was cotton shawls and prayer.

Girls of 12 with listless faces hung around the night streets. Prostitution has not disappeared from Mexico, but it is better fed and clothed, not quite as hungry and diffident, not quite as *young*. In a savagely beautiful land I found the expensive mixture of people speaking fifty different languages was ruled by a race of amiable but moody trigger-men, attempting to feed and house the ever-growing tide of humanity which washes against the borders of the capital.

Violence continues to rage across Mexico. The drugs war is out of control. Last year some 6,000 Mexicans were victims of drugs-related murders. Traffickers are armed with AK-47 assault rifles as well as the heavier 50mm calibre weapons known as 'police killers'. In one weekend in southern Mexico twelve people were gunned down, including a policeman and six children—more than 800 drugs-related murders in one month.

I started filming in Mexico City at Easter, and was flung into the deep end of this fervently religious—though officially atheist—country. We went to film the Crucifixion at Ixtapalapa, joining the crowd of a quarter of a million watching this passion play. It could have been just such a crowd upon a dusty hillside at that other Calvary—a smouldering mass full of awe and violence. Pickpockets ferreted through the crush and tourists were warned to keep away.

We had unusual protection: I had organized a truck with an armed escort, and filmed from its open back amid the tumult. As we struggled to repel boarders, our government Man from the Ministry waved his gun about quite effectively, threatening anyone. I think he came from Public Relations.

Our day had begun at dawn, in peace, but already the promise of turbulence hung upon the shimmering air. The morning sun fell upon a raggle-taggle brass band as it spread its unique sound across the growing mass of worshippers— and helmeted police stood ready with tear gas. In the hot dust, amid realism heightened by a harsh and arid landscape and by emotion, we waited to see the trial of Christ, the procession to Calvary, the Crucifixion . . .

Easter at Ixtapalapa is no simple demonstration of faith and religious conviction, for beneath the elemental medieval Christianity of a complex people an ancient pagan tradition survives. They have a straightforward habit of taking mysteries literally: a congregation will send a Virgin Mary back to heaven rather quickly—with the help of a rocket ...

The Mexicans are extremely proud and courteous, poetic and cruel, merry and violent. They regard the Cross as a potent symbol of the old magic calendar. It is not an abstraction but is itself a wonder-working god. All the ancients of Central America worship that Cross, which as a Christian symbol may also be invoked by pagans.

So before he was an agonized Christ in his crown of thorns, he was an employee of the local office of the Ministry of Justice. With the two barefaced thieves, he was scourged through the streets. This was no gentle Oberammergau. There was little play-acting in the intolerable burden of the Cross. Led through dust clouds by penitents, the three slowly climbed the arid rocky hill which was the site of one of the most significant Aztec ceremonies every fifty-two years, when the end of the world was awaited and priests sacrificed an honoured victim, building a fire in the cavity from which they had just ripped out his heart.

As a visitor—indeed an honoured victim—this was not a comfortable day of filming. I could not find out how near we were to the ending of the ominous fifty-two years when the world stopped, but it hung over the day. I absorbed the worshippers closely, ready to detect any change of attitude towards *this* victim. How we would have escaped from that crowded hillside I could not imagine. If the worshippers changed their attitude, we would last a few minutes.

The Aztecs, distant ancestors of the men we

were filming, were a colourful and lusty race. The violent pageantry and the religious ceremonies could only be matched, perhaps, by the solemn ferocity of inquisitional Christianity. When the Church turned to kindliness and paternal beneficence, to concern by Christian example, the Indians—the would-be converts—missed the violence and orgiastic release of their old religion. Sometimes they would slip away for a surreptitious rain dance in veneration of their old god, Tlaloc.

So the good friars, tempering their Christianity with practicality, decided to put a little more zing into their piety. They allowed Mexicans to adapt the Catholic hagiography to their own taste and colours, their own sense of drama, their memory of the terror a deity *ought* to inspire.

Religion elsewhere in the world can become a weekly investment in peace of mind which need not intrude upon the practicalities of everyday life. In Mexico it is a central tragedy—the very core of pain and humility, the altar of guilt and self-effacement.

Moaning peasants approached the shrine upon their knees, with heads, necks, waists and ankles strung with spicy cactus leaves that tear the skin. At Ixtapalapa they were venerating the god who destroyed their own gods, banished the smoking mirror, the hummingbird wizard, the feathered serpent. They had come to worship the greatest god of all, whose soldiers broke the old images, the god who for the first time did not exact human sacrifice but instead sacrificed himself.

It is impossible for most Mexican Indians to regard Catholic deities as distant, inscrutable beings. In some areas they are still on probation, aliens who may just possibly turn out to possess unusual power. After more than five centuries of Christianity they still treat their saints as idols.

As we stood in our truck amid the awestruck mass, we wondered whether the struggling figure before us, toiling up the hillside beneath the weight of the Cross, was seen by the worshipping, moaning, ecstatic crowd as God or man or idol. All those taking part in that procession were living roles that had been handed down from generation to generation. Each Indian centurion, hot in his red velvet cloak, retained his family's role. The intensity of their fervour created a disquieting air of reality.

I was uncomfortably aware that all through southern Mexico there remain traces of a cult, a thin stream of memory or fanaticism which centres upon the Indian Christ, a dark Christ who was crucified *for* the Indians. Both Mayas and Zatapec Indians have offered themselves for actual crucifixion on such days, a right carried out in deepest secrecy and reverence. They reason: 'The Christ who died far away across the seas was rejected by his own people. He did not know the Indians. But if one of us died upon the cross of his own will, then we can be sure this sacrifice was truly made for us.'

So token crucifixions have become fatally real and peasants have been nailed to the cross they carried, to die upon a hill before a reverent mass.

After those tortuous and intense days on Ixtapalapa, we escaped with relief to a fiesta, and there is no better place to forget the terrors of the hereafter and the frustrations of the now than at the San Marcos Fair at Aguascalientes, most

93

famous of all Mexico's festivals. The state is on the central plateau at a height of 1,800 metres. It was a long day's drive to get there from the capital, and of course when we arrived there was no room at the inn. We bedded down, gratefully, in the hotel lobby.

When we began to film the fiesta, we were constantly told that some French photographer in the crowd wanted to meet us. I had quite enough to worry about—but he turned out to be the great Henri Cartier-Bresson, taking pictures for a book. After that he travelled with us and shamed my cameraman by being twice his age and twice as active.

The fiesta, Mexico's highest expression of social life, proved the most shapeless, most ragged of combustions—a happy explosion of the communal soul. Festivals are always breaking out somewhere in Mexico, because every day belongs to some saint. For run-of-the-mill saints, fiestas last a day or two; very miraculous saints are saluted for a week. St Mark was acknowledged at Aguascalientes by two weeks of carnival. The texture of his nights was thick—a heady tropical mixture of heat, sweat and religion, and the endless assault of the deafening noise all Mexicans love.

It was a brilliant reversal of the reticence and silence of their ordinary lives, and one of the rare occasions when the Mexican opened out to the world—shouting, dancing and firing his pistol in the air. Men who have exchanged only formal courtesies during the past year will now trade confidences, get deeply drunk, discover they are brothers—and on occasion, go on to kill each

94

other . . . At such an event the flashpoint of the average Mexican is as low as can be.

As a foreigner exposed to such dangerous amiability, I faced the nice judgement of how chummy to get with a group of befuddled characters who wanted to be friendly—and carried knives in case their friendship was spurned. There was the further anxiety of just how much one could drink and remain safe socially, as well as internally.

There was always the unforeseen but deadly insult of looking too long at some young woman— or in some cases, of not looking long enough!

The risk of a sudden outflow of personal blood was increased by the presence of our cameras. This delighted some, but confused and infuriated others.

Despite many attempts around the world to impose views and attitudes upon me, despite revolutionaries, police, politicians, bureaucrats and pressure groups, I have never submitted the content of any programme to censorship, but St Mark's carnival would be harder to deny.

We had now been casually introduced to a teacher of English, a rather seedy little man out of Graham Greene who leeched on to us and offered his help as interpreter. We tolerated him as a grey and shadowy sponger until, when we were filming one night amid noisy excitement and having a little local difficulty with some policeman, our unctuous little interpreter forgot himself. He flashed a badge which caused all the officers and everyone else to step back a pace. It apparently revealed him as a powerful officer of the State Secret Police. We all went rather quiet and thoughtful.

First we had to try and remember what he had

seen and overheard. Then we had to take evasive action to make sure he was decoyed whenever we filmed or recorded anything that might upset him and his superiors.

Though no doubt he could have called for thumbscrews and clanging cell doors, he was not very frightening. When we finally left town he presented me with some ashtrays stolen from a restaurant, and suggested the size of his tip. May *all* our secret policemen be as mild!

Never to be forgotten in Mexico is the need for every man to prove himself very male—preferably by some outrageous and pointless show of courage. If he can't find a bull, he can demonstrate this by driving his car through the red lights, by knifing someone who could have affronted him, by establishing a *casa chica* he can't afford, by siring a great number of children. There are endless ways, large and small, but always, and above all things, every *hombre* must be *macho*.

How does one explain Mexico's annual sport: the bullfight? Deep-grained Indian pride and fatalism, perhaps. The adoration of blood and death, common to Aztecs and Spaniards. The years of conquest and cruel class distinction. Such displays of excessive strength grew painfully out of debilities and guilts, out of mixed blood, hunger and unemployment and a knowledge that through the centuries he has always been tricked and judged, first by foreigners, then by his countrymen. The outcome, caught in the defiance and narcissism of the bullfight, is a fragile ego, a violent pride, a low flashpoint and one of the highest murder rates in the world. It also shows itself in great charm and gallantry and courage. It is inescapable.

So unfortunately is *la mordida,* 'the bite', which over the centuries has become an established national practice.

Certainly money talks everywhere in the world, but in Mexico it does so rather more simply and openly, from the traffic policemen who lean on motorists, through unpaid bureaucrats who must be bribed before anything happens and count such bribes as part of their salaries, to the minister who may demand a 20 per cent kickback on the cost of building a dam. It is expected and accepted that most politicians will emerge from office very rich indeed. Resigned and envious Mexicans in the street merely hope that while indulging themselves, they may help the country too. Sometimes, very rarely, they do.

Indeed the Mexican attitude to death is very different to ours, as was shown by the gruesome mummies we filmed in the catacombs of old and battered Guanajuato, which are still regularly visited in a friendly fashion by relatives—like popping round the corner to see Gran.

Mexicans have an awareness that life is the preparation for death, the other half of death. Life may be short and sick and dismal, but death is long. That at least is certain, so the Mexican displays his coming death as an adornment, a jewel. To us death is no joking matter. In Mexico the idea of dying can have something luminous about it—something almost light-hearted. At first sight the attitude seems playful.

To prepare for All Saints Day, the Day of the Dead, Mexican women bake the Bread of the Dead, fashioning shrouded, appetizing, sweetly

97

smiling corpses, all crisply cinnamoned and glazed. Children walk around munching skulls made of sugar and marked with their own names, or gobbling up chocolate skeletons.

This national holiday seems a sort of macabre carnival, for there are few Mexican families which do not make a pilgrimage to the cemeteries to picnic around the graves of dead relatives, made pretty by candles and flowers. Marigolds are most popular for they are the traditional Aztec flowers of the dead. Happily mourning families light their candles and begin their night vigil, eating and exchanging recollections of the person whose grave they are using as a picnic table. The cemeteries seem to cover a legion of will-o'-the-wisp—a phosphorescent light that flares from the earth on marshy ground.

In Mexico the grave is *not* a fine and private place. They sit celebrating in their cemeteries until dawn during this bleak carnival. The living may not always be fully at ease on such eerie occasions but the dead are supposed to enjoy them very much indeed.

To the Indians, all dead are the subject of real and continuous concern. In southern Mexico where people still regard death as the beginning of an actual three-year journey to the next world, they believe that though their souls are 'in glory' they still have human feelings. Their favourite food and drink are offered, the songs they liked best are sung. Women wear their Sunday clothes and brightest necklaces and children are kept on their best behaviour, exactly as though an honoured guest were in the home.

Next day, after the visited dead have enjoyed the

'essence' of the proffered food by inhaling its odour and extracting its flavour, it may be eaten by the household which provided it. In Oaxaca there is a further charming tradition of hospitality to poor old souls who have no families to return to, no one to entertain them upon their return visit. Separate candles are lit for them and offerings spread, so no solitary soul need feel lonely during the general reunion.

For days before and after this Day of the Dead, death is everywhere present. Death-bread leers invitingly from bakery windows. In sweet shops, candy skulls have bright tinsel eyes. At toy shops children beg for little coffins out of which, at the tug of a string, jump tiny skeletons. *Señoritas* present their boyfriends with skeleton tiepins. Throughout Mexico all death joins in daily life, macabre but familiar and not fearful. 'If I must die tomorrow,' they sing with yearning, 'why not at once—today?'

They believe that by intense prayer and sacrifice they might be able to keep their gods kindly disposed. All mankind had to pray together so that its clock might keep ticking. Individual death, the Aztecs believed, was not destruction but transformation—so handsome young warriors went happily to the sacrificial slab. It was reasoned that for man to survive, the gods which permitted his existence must also wax strong, so they receive the best nutriments, the most precious offerings from the very heart of man, wrenched by priests from living bodies. At the dedication of one Aztec temple 20,000 people were sacrificed. Some were skinned and sometimes their arms and legs were eaten.

So in Mexico, where peasants bury their dead as though planting seeds, death has been domesticated, the skull turned into a popular decoration, the corpses of friends and relations carefully preserved. This familiarity, this intimacy with death that we avoid, does not necessarily mean fearlessness; it could mean a dread that demands elaborate propitiation.

To find death at the door
Is no less awesome for Mexicans
But in Mexico it knocks more often
And must more frequently be admitted

12

EASY TO TEACH WOMEN TO SHOOT, HARDER TO TEACH THEM TO *KILL*

In an early *Whicker's World* around Texas I wondered whether my conviction that every Texan carried a hidden gun could possibly be accurate. So I went out with my cameras into the monstrous avenues of Houston, stopped passers-by and asked whether they owned a gun. I very soon discovered it was not a question of yes or no, but of how many.

A couple of gentle nuns carried their handgun in the glove box of the convent car. A priest said he wouldn't feel safe without his. A newspaper seller had a dozen handguns. Frontier justice was instantly available, on all sides.

The right to carry arms is at the very core of the

American Constitution, as we've seen in thousands of Westerns. In Texas, of course, weapons of self-defence were always vital, from the frontier days.

I thought maybe the proliferation of handguns I discovered might be merely because we were in the wild state of Texas, so I waited until I got to urban California to check again.

In Beverly Hills I visited Juliet Mills, most English of actresses. This daughter of the late Sir John was living in typical Beverly Hills style in a large mansion with a basement shooting range, guarded by a couple of Alsatians and, most emphatically, by her then husband Michael Miklenda. A Czech and gun enthusiast, he always carried a handgun in a shoulder holster even, he told me, under his dinner jacket.

He opened a display case of guns. It was like Tiffany's, only more dazzling. When he went away, he said, he stored the best guns in his bank vault and booby-trapped the rest.

Juliet explained, 'All our close friends—I'd say about 75 per cent of them—have a gun and know how to use it, especially any woman who lives alone. She'd be crazy not to protect herself. I certainly do.'

Yet today such law-abiding householders must face not only the danger of being robbed, raped or murdered by intruders, but of being sued by them. Juliet recalled a mutual friend who one night found to her horror that she had an armed intruder inside her home. She had been taught to use her bedside gun, so before he could shoot she beat him to the draw in High Noon style and, as he ran away, shot him again. He was wounded, but still on his feet.

Now this armed punk with a long police record was taking her to court, and she would surely be punished for defending herself against whatever it was he wanted to do.

The police, when they arrived, reminded her that three quarters of any intruder's body had to be inside her home when he was shot.

In his slight Middle European accent Michael recalled another most emphatic way of handling the problem. 'Here in Beverly Hills, just nearby, a friend of mine was burgled. He knew about guns, so he caught the burglar and had him with his hands up against the wall. He held his gun over the burglar while he dialled the police. The burglar said, "What are you doing?" He said, "I'm calling the cops, and they'll come and get you." The guy was laughing. He said, "You do that, you just do that. I'll get about six months, max. Then I'll come back—and I'll *kill* you. I know where you live."'

'This made my friend think twice. He could see that every dark night when he came home to his wife and kids he was going to worry whether this guy was out there behind some bush in the garden. This year, next year . . . there'd always be that threat of a shot in the night hanging over his family . . .

'So he made up his mind. He could hear the police phone ringing as he put it down, clicked his gun—and shot the guy, shot him dead. The police came and took the body away. That was that. End of story.'

It was not the 'end of story' for me; the memory of that strange shot in the night has never left me.

One evening I went to a gun school in Glendale where Alex Goodrich, hospital carpenter and

102

marksman, ran a self-protection course. Most of the class were frightened women, doing something about it—housewives and nurses, secretaries and shop assistants, actresses and stewardesses, even doctors and lawyers who were so frightened that they were eager to go back to a school of a very different kind.

'It's easy to teach women to shoot,' he told me, 'but it's harder to teach them to kill.' In a state where anyone can buy a gun and gun shops ran weekly 'specials', one frightened girl admitted, 'Shooting somebody—it's called survival.'

Shooting at the next target that evening was a quiet, soft-spoken doctor who was supporting his wife. He had been almost killed by a passing hoodlum who shot him in the hospital car park for the drugs in his attaché case. His wife said, 'I've always hated guns, and would never be in this class except for the fact that my husband was shot and almost died. If I'd had a gun I'm sure I could have driven this hoodlum away.'

This is the dark side of life in sunny California. It is the price they pay for living in the most free and casual country, where refusal to forget the Wild West and banish their guns means that around 10,000 Americans are shot every year. Alex Goodrich tells his class, 'If you miss, you're going to die. It's that simple. I have to turn you peaceful people into instant killers.'

Elegant homes now sprout steel shutters, alarms, electrified fences; some are patrolled by private armies. Every man his own Sundance. One student, a nurse, was in a car park and about to drive home when she was accosted by a flasher who walked around exposing himself. He stood by her car, trying to get her to show interest.

She took her gun from the glove box and aimed it—and was interested to watch a record detumescence.

The gun-toting hero has always been glorified in California, but now in a time of paranoia he is reinforced from the ranks of the victims, the prey, who agonize about staying alive. Today, the threatening shadow cast across the world's most ridiculed, most envied outpost is the everyday dread of casual violence. Los Angeles lost its innocence forty years ago after the mass killings by the Charles Manson family, yet the crime rate is bolstered by thousands of Mexicans—all poor, many on drugs—who cross the border illegally to compound the problems of this good-living city, its rash of crime, its bizarre and motiveless murders.

In the meaner streets of San Francisco I went to see Carol and Russell O'Rea who ran one of the most popular targets for armed hoodlums and junkies hunting for cash at night: a liquor store and gun shop. They were more experienced in gun culture than they looked. Their drab store on the main road to the Bridge was distinctive only because of the bullet holes around its walls.

Both were in their 60s, he heavy and lugubrious, she a smiling bespectacled little old gran—but it seems that, in California, little old ladies can take care of themselves. 'This fellow, a white fellow, came in one night. Nobody around, just me and him. I was kind of jittery,' she says. 'He wanted a pack of Camels, and when I went to pick them up I could see that under the counter he had a 9mm German Luger automatic . . . I tell you, I just froze.

'He says, "Get down on the floor." He was such a mean-looking thing. I got down, and under the counter we had a 38/40, you know, one of those large old-fashioned guns, and I thought, Gee, this has to be, I've got to do something. It's him or me . . . So I put my finger in the trigger and—*bang*! I shot him right between the eyes.

'Still there's nobody around, nobody heard me, so I thought, Oh heck, I'll take another chance and shoot him—so I shot him in the neck—and down he went. I walked around, I wanted to get a towel to wipe his face because he was bleeding so bad. He'd only taken $39. I went to search his pockets to get my $39 back.

'I couldn't find it, but I saw his neck moving, so I ran outside and shot in the air, thinking maybe someone might say, "Look at that crazy person," and come over. Nothing. So I dial the operator. I says, "You'd better call the police," I says, "because I think I killed somebody." "Hold on," she says, and before I knew it I had seven cop cars and television and everything—here! He was on the floor, but he was already dead.

'So I says, "Listen," I says, "take that money out of his pocket, he's got my $39" . . . and it was *bloody*. I put it in the cash register, and they took him away. I had dum-dum bullets, you know, they enter the skull and fly into hundreds of pieces, just pulverize the brain.'

So you didn't really need that second shot?

'No I didn't, I just wanted to see how it feels!'

Was it the first time you'd killed anybody?

'There's been a few more—about four—but I shoot twice, that's all I shoot. Third time I don't shoot. If I can't get them in those two, I quit . . .'

13

A POM WHO'S MADE GOOD—
IF THAT'S THE WORD

Mrs Dorrie Flatman, a hairdresser from Lyelake Road, Kirkby, Liverpool, sailed for Australia in 1963, taking her three daughters and £45. She has now lived in Perth, Western Australia, for some forty years and is certainly a Pom who's made good—if that's the word.

Running three flourishing businesses, she seemed a pillar of the establishment, well known around town, dressed expensively by Louis Féraud, married to Kim, an accountant twenty-one years younger—younger indeed than her three daughters. They were quite prominent on the Perth social scene, attending fashion shows, appearing in the gossip columns, giving to charity—for Mrs Flatman had a handsome income.

Dorrie was very wealthy indeed, and was a proper little madam. On my last visit, some twenty years ago, she was running three of Perth's sixteen tolerated brothels. In those days her girls could earn A$2,000 a week, which in each case meant another $2,000 for Dorrie, who got half the take.

I was making a series of programmes about Brits who had emigrated to Australia and made good, so this story sounded classic Dick Whittington. On my arrival in Perth I tried to locate her. Everyone had heard of Mrs Flatman, but no one was prepared to admit that they knew the whereabouts of her establishments. They all clammed up. I was finally advised to go to I Capricci, the smartest boutique in town, and make enquiries as she was a sharp dresser and big spender. Yes, they knew a Mrs Flatman, she was a good customer with exceptional taste.

They didn't want to talk about her, but I got a phone number and suggested a meeting. Polite but cautious, she agreed to come to my hotel with her husband.

A few minutes before they were due to arrive Valerie went down to the lobby to post a letter. She came back in the lift with an unusual couple: a slender woman in her 60s with short orange hair, and a much younger, dark-haired man. Valerie watched, transfixed, as the man carefully wound a wire around his waist and slipped a tape-recorder into an inside pocket. It was Mr and Mrs Flatman, heading for our suite,and if that was a clandestine recording they weren't very good at it!

Forewarned that everything said might be taken down and used in evidence against me, I welcomed them gently, and we settled down for an agreeable conversation about her business. She was surprisingly forthcoming and straightforward, and quite unabashed by her oldest profession. We agreed to meet again next day, this time at one of her houses. I asked how I'd find it, and she looked surprised. 'Every taxi driver knows where I am,' she said. She was right.

Her main establishment in Perth was a neat, carefully anonymous building with thirteen bedrooms on a main road just outside the city centre, its front door always half open. Behind it, a cash desk displayed all the credit cards, among them, I noticed, Barclaycard. The client, if seen to be acceptable, passed through a remote-controlled door into a suburban sitting room, more Maples than bordello, where the television was always on.

She gave me a tour of her house with thirteen bedrooms. She employed the same interior decorator as the Perth Hilton, and was happy to show off the themed rooms: African, Egyptian, Roman, and her special ground-floor facilities for the handicapped. Her pride and joy was a jacuzzi. 'I can get seven in there with ease,' she said proudly.

The routine for interviewing our madam was relaxed and made commonplace. Every day we would have a late breakfast, then drive over and spend the day amidst the coming and going of one of her brothels. It began to feel quite normal. Dorrie was so open, unselfconscious and matter-of-fact that it would have been easy to believe that she was running a responsible public service. The whole process was disarming.

She ran her business much as she would have run a chain store: listening to what the customers wanted and making sure she could provide it. 'You have to cater for all tastes,' she said, explaining that in a brothel personality was more important than looks. It wasn't always the prettiest who were the money-makers. Men often preferred plainer girls, in the belief that they would make more of an effort to please. I had noticed this, in Dorrie's domain.

Like any efficient businesswoman, she knew her market: Greeks and Italians liked fat girls, Asians wanted slim blondes. The clientele was varied.

British and Australian sailors never had enough money, and much of her lucrative Japanese trade had been lost to casinos. There were the regulars who came from all walks of life: lonely immigrants, frustrated husbands, pensioners, doctors and lawyers. And there were the ground-floor clients: men in wheelchairs or too old to make it up the stairs.

Of all the nationalities catered for, the worst were the Macedonians. 'They tend to treat their women a bit rough,' said Dorrie. 'If they pay for something they think they own it, that kind of thing. They're very very rough in the room. If a girl finds somebody too rough, she's got a panic button near the bed. She'll press it and the whole lot of us will be up the stairs two at a time. If the door's locked, we've got one master key that'll open every door. There's safety in numbers, which is why girls tend to come to a brothel to work, instead of on their own.'

Every now and then a bell summoned the girls on duty for consideration. They'd dash down the hallway in their lingerie and leotards, chattering, and encourage the waiting men with smiles and polite but restrained conversation. Those not chosen and taken upstairs returned to the kitchen, picked up their knitting, removed their suppers from the microwave and talked about their children. Their cosy domestic scene had only briefly been interrupted. Most of the men were so unattractive that rejection by them, you would have thought, would have been a relief!

Presiding over this anthology of pros, Dorrie, with her matter-of-fact tenacity and Liverpool commonsense would, I suspect, have been a success in almost any business. She was brisk, no-nonsense, ready to answer directly any question you could think of about her esoteric life.

She took great care with her appearance, dressing at the best boutique, dieting carefully, putting aside three mornings a week with a hairdresser and one for aromatherapy and a facial. She had recently submitted to operations upon both her eyes to improve her sight, and had been able to discard her heavy glasses.

For relaxation she visited the Perth Casino—on Saturday afternoons. In the old days she took her 83-year-old mother. Her husband Kim was a boyish bank clerk contemplating life as a missionary when he married into a three-brothel family and lived happily ever after. He now looked after Dorrie's double-entry bookkeeping and also did most of the cooking in their large house on one of Perth's better estates. Every day he collected her from her place of work in a flash red sports car, and drove home to prepare supper.

She was strict with the girls, but fair and sympathetic, more matron of an unruly girls' school than Diamond Lil, and the lack of glitz made the establishment peculiarly Australian. She and the girls liked to think of prostitution as a job like any other, working shifts, keeping office hours, paying tax. There were rules and regulations, but, most importantly, they must look after their clients. Bad language was unacceptable. Any girl caught swearing would be asked to empty her locker and leave. 'If you talk to clients like a lady, they'll treat you like a lady. You get no trouble in a house if you behave correctly. You may be a prostitute but you can still be a lady.'

Dorrie's was very much a family business. When I was there, Bridie McFarrell was one of her 'sitters'—the women who manage brothels. Once upon a time, back in Liverpool, she had been a *babysitter* for Dorrie. Now, after a chance meeting in Australia, the soft-spoken abandoned wife ran her branch brothel in Fremantle where, in those days, they had not yet painted over the sign indicating the establishment's previous use: The Fremantle Fitness Centre. 'Wrong exercises!' said Bridie.

She and the other sitters controlled a happy horde of harlots, a fanfare of strumpets whose numbers fluctuated between forty-five and twenty-five girls in Dorrie's three houses, which operated three shifts.

Generally the girls were bright and cheerful. Bridie told me that to kill time they sometimes played Charades—there's wicked for you. Their looks were commonplace—at best—but most were articulate and sympathetic. I frequently found it quite hard to avoid asking the standard, 'What's a nice girl like you . . . ?'

I found the romanticized idea of the golden-hearted whore hard to believe—but Dorrie was adamant that most of the girls were soft-hearted and kind. They felt sorry for their clients, specially the lonely misfits, sometimes even feeling guilty taking money from them. 'There are a few girls who come into the business because they can't be bothered to do a normal job, but others come with a purpose: they've got families to keep, they are single mothers, deserted housewives, people saving up to buy a home. I like the single mothers because they've got a reason to work and they are reliable. And if a girl comes in here and says, "I want to buy a house," she's got an aim and you know she's going to be a good worker.

'You have to understand the girls and be a mother to them, listen to them and not be hard on them. A girl may have ten clients a day and she's got to make each of them feel that he's the one she's been waiting for—and it's not an easy job.'

Many of these working girls—as they're called internationally—had been prostitutes most of their adult lives. They leave occasionally to rejoin the straight world, but usually drift back again. They see their daily chores as just another job and, once the heavy make-up has been washed away and the street clothes put on, they slip back easily into everyday anonymity.

Their drug is money. Once they had got used to that daily wad of dollars from the house reception desk as they went off shift—tax already deducted—it became almost impossible to contemplate eight hours in an office or a shop for a tenth of that reward.

A good-looking Scots girl had been working for Dorrie for a year. The money, she said, was addictive. She had intended just to work for a few weeks before Christmas but being a compulsive spender her earnings were so good she couldn't give it up. 'I like nice things. Once you've had the $200 dress you don't want the $20 dress.' Her husband had no idea what she did for a living, and she swore that if her children found out she'd kill herself. Once out of the house and in normal street clothes she never gave her job a second thought, though she did admit that she used to

112

have a great sex life with her husband but that now, somehow, things were not quite the same.

I watched as a Chinese client arrived demanding someone younger and prettier, someone who didn't look like a prostitute. The girls were surprisingly patient with him. 'You're looking for a supermodel. That sort of girl doesn't do escort work, she'd spit in your eye.' He left, looking crushed. They were happier with the arrival of the Japanese navy *en masse,* popular customers who were clean and easy to please. With the prospect of a busy weekend ahead a huge consignment of condoms arrived. The girls had made a special order for their Asian customers; one size, apparently, doesn't fit all.

So they did their time in Dorrie's parlours, dreaming of an uncomplicated future with a family in some suburban home—which was always a year or two ahead. Meanwhile, in their fantasy world, they waited patiently and cheerfully for real life to begin.

Some 200 girls work in Perth's sixteen contained brothels, with another 120 operating outside the system. They are tolerated, provided they follow certain simple rules: no underage girls, no drugs, no men at all involved in their operation . . . Australian police have found containment the ideal way of keeping the lid on prostitution among a city population of about a million, so madams of approved brothels, like Dorrie, can operate securely within a closed shop and be protected by the police—if not by the law.

One evening I had drinks with Dorrie in her comfortable home with its syncopated musical door chimes, pot plants and frilly lace curtains.

Dressed in a printed silk dress she was about to give a birthday party for one of her girls. Her treat was an outing to Collars and Cuffs, a male strip club where the Full Monty was *de rigeur.* It sounded more like a busman's holiday.

Dorrie's second marriage was as unusual as her profession. Kim came from a religious background; unable to persuade his new wife to accompany him to Borneo, his missionary zeal had evaporated. His parents had been less than enthusiastic at the prospect of a daughter-in-law with children older than their son, when they still believed she was a hairdresser. Now he kept the brothels' books in order and was scrupulous about the girls' tax returns, claiming relief for fishnet stockings and underwear as tools of trade.

Dorrie loved her work. For her, it was a vocation. She was never bored, she met a great variety of people, and even when she had what she termed hairy-scary moments when she'd been chased by the authorities she was unfazed. She could cope with most things. When threatened by a gang demanding protection money she had calmly called the police, warning the crims, 'If you're not out of that door in two minutes, you'll go through it head first.' They fled.

Her problems were peculiar to her profession: protecting her girls from violent men, turning away drunks, finding a discipline mistress who enjoyed the work—but not *too* much. She must not beat him to a pulp. Dorrie took it all in her stride between visits to the hairdresser and considered herself to be a most respectable madam. She is now over 80, and celebrated her last birthday at an up-market Perth restaurant with Kim and her daughters. The occasion was noted in all the gossip columns of the local papers. I'm sure she was pleased.

14

A MOST SIGNIFICANT PINNACLE OF CORAL

Before I set off for the smallest, richest republic in the world, I could find no one who had even *heard* of the place, let alone visited it—until I landed upon this dot in the Pacific, 26 miles south of the Equator and close to nowhere. It was hidden in the South Seas some 2,500 miles from Tokyo and Sydney and Honolulu and everywhere else, lonely and lost.

I joined 3,500 islanders, with the same number of outsiders who work for them—or more precisely, stand in for them in their ultimate welfare state. They pay no taxes at all and enjoy free housing, free telephones, free hospitals, free education— even free buses to take them to work, should they ever feel like doing any. For these amiable islanders, work is something other people do.

The home island is about two miles by three and, in the vast Pacific, easy to miss. You can drive round its one road in twenty minutes in the Mercedes you've just been given, and meet yourself coming back—unless you'd prefer a speedboat, this time? Yet their sweltering speck of equatorial Gilbert-and-Sullivan has the most unusual concentration of wealth in the world. The name of this parched tropical dot? Nauru.

115

When I was there the Nauruans, per head, had more credit in the bank than the Kuwaitis or the Swiss, and that's before the crunch. Certainly they made *us* look like poor relations—which sadly we are; Nauru is a special member of the Commonwealth. They have no harbour, but are buildinga merchant fleet of six ships. They are also building a £13 million 47-storey skyscraper in Melbourne.

I went there at the start of a tour of the South Seas, flying (of course) Air Nauru. Yes indeed, with the population of an English village, Nauru has its own airline—and don't think the aircraft is some tired old Dakota or fluttery Tiger Moth. This was a £2 million 66-seater Fellowship jet, with all first-class seating. It was later exchanged for a Boeing 737-400. Then (first sign of shrinkage?) a 737-300.

During my first visit in 1972 I had interviewed the island's splendidly named founding President Hammer deRoburt, in the days when Nauru had the highest living standard in the Pacific. This time I travelled south from Hong Kong, through Brisbane and Sydney, to catch this swish little airliner in Melbourne, because that's the boarding point at the end of the line. We promptly flew north again, back through Brisbane and on towards the Equator and the world's smallest independent republic, to Air Nauru's homeland— a most significant speck of coral, which started as bird droppings.

They haven't lost the common touch. When I went to call on the President, I got a message delaying my visit for an hour. His butler had a late night, so Mr President had to do thetidying up himself.

With no soil to speak of, drab little Nauru is no tropical garden. No fishing, no fruit, almost no rain—and the hungriest mosquitoes I've chased. Its people have a reputation for being dour—'the Scots of the Pacific'. Certainly they are not among the world's workers, or always welcoming. They refused to admit a BBC *24 Hours* television team, leaving them kicking their heels in New Guinea, and very cross. Those visitors who are admitted must have visas and return tickets. With some justification, Nauruans fear commercial exploitation—though the Côte d'Azur it's *not*.

From the President down, I found them most agreeable—if not noticeably talented. Strangely for Polynesians, they neither sing nor dance. On high days and holidays the Gilbert and Ellice islanders, who work for them, also *sing* for them. They have no written language. They don't paint or weave or carve wood. Their only craft—not a particularly exciting one—is the making of string figures: cats' cradles. What shall we do *tomorrow* night?

They do, however, have one extraordinary custom which I have found nowhere else in the world. Called *bubutsi*, it means that on certain days and holidays you can go into any islander's house and *bubutsi* anything you covet—help yourself to a bed or a car, a radio or a speedboat. Admire it—then take it home. The owner will merely look resigned as you drive away. Next time he'll probably do you. It's the most direct way of redistributing wealth, though not much fun for the rich folk.

Bubutsi is no joke, however. Families have been

bubutsied into poverty. One house was stripped; a wealthy man told me he was unsure how to defend himself against those who may have decided to strip his home next time. He was planning to put all his valuables in one locked room, and then try to convince predators he had lost the key! This struck me as a very poor effort at defence, when even the Mercedes of the President's wife's had been *bubutsied.* You need to know who's who—but of course on a tiny isle that's not too difficult. I was interviewing a gang of Hell's Angels on their Harleys when one told me he was also a member of the island's police force.

So how come they're so rich? Well, they've proved once again that where there's muck, there's money. Their tiny island is almost entirely composed of a congealed brown dust formed, in the depths of time, by bird droppings . . . and supported by decomposed fish. There's romance for you. An elementary birth for what has become a very valuable substance indeed.

It wasn't enough for such expensive muck just to lie there; it needed the preparation of the ages. In the course of time the whole island has twice been beneath the Pacific for a few centuries, but now Nauru's up in the world again, its brown dust prepared and ready for delivery.

It is almost pure phosphate, this fertilizer sold to enrich the world's fields—a ready international market. At the end of every two months Nauruan landowners just collect their National Phosphate Company dividend cheques—and start spending!

Nauru's economy depends almost entirely on those declining phosphate deposits. There are few other resources. Even necessities must be imported. For a while, Nauru survived as a tax haven, but there wasn't enough action.

These Polynesians have some odd ways of using their time. Would you prefer Hell's Angels—or WeightWatchers? I filmed both. A determined Angel could get right round the island's road (singular) in fifteen minutes and, with a population of fewer than 10,000, who are you watching your weight for? Hard to decide where to go tomorrow.

Now here comes the bad news: Nauru's 100-million tons of phosphate were worked out in 2006. The faster they export the good earth, the less there is to stand on. Their homeland gets smaller and excavation leaves only an environmental wasteland—coral pinnacles in a lunar graveyard in which nothing can grow.

The value of its Government Trust recently shrank from A$1,300 million to A$138 million, and carried on down. As a result of heavy spending from Nauru's trust funds, the National Bank of Nauru is insolvent and the government faces bankruptcy. The Australian dollar is Nauru's official currency, and recently the island has provided Australia with the prison location for locking up illegal immigrants and asylum seekers. This could prove a nice little earner.

As though Nauru didn't have enough problems, it was persuaded to invest £2 million in a London musical, which was a disaster. Called *Leonardo,* it was a massive flop and closed after five weeks— one of the biggest disasters in the history of the London theatre.

The amiable island has an uncertain future. With no source of income apart from bird droppings, it remains a poor but happy Micawberesque

119

paradise, waiting for something to turn up—perhaps other shiploads of bird muck? The island has a few years of life before it becomes uninhabitable . . . unless the filthy rich Nauruans reverse the process—and *import* dirt!

There are no personal taxes in Nauru, though it's hoped that the sale of deep-sea fishing rights may generate some revenue. Or possibly Australian millionaires feeling the need for space. After all, they've got 40 million square miles to occupy.

Nauru has . . . eight.

15

THAT'S FOR THE RELEVANT DEMON-GIANT TO WORRY ABOUT

Everything you ever heard about Bali . . . is true. For a start, it's perfect. Unique among the dreamaway places of the world, Bali's a lilting pageant of temples and festivals. The island is one huge botanical garden, pervaded by a sort of enchantment where copper-skinned Balinese drift through their improbable never-never-land . . . Not just a magic isle, but an experience, a sensation.

Few places in the world have been officially designated 'a paradise', but that's Bali's fate. International agencies have pronounced that, like oil or uranium, copper or coal, the natural beauty of this isle is a marketable commodity, ripe for further exploitation.

At its heart is Mount Agung, the holy mountain that is also an active volcano—nothing here

120

escapes religious significance. Then in 1963 this revered mountain in *un*holy eruption killed 1,600 and left 87,000 homeless.

In an area notorious for disaster, famine and revolution, Bali's the ornament of tropical Asia, despite occasional ferocity during elections. A third the size of Yorkshire, it's only 80 miles by 50—the kind of place that, like Brigadoon, could vanish if you looked away. Part of it did disappear, most cruelly, on 12 October 2002 when three bombers blew open the tourist district of Kuta, around Paddy's Pub. It was the deadliest act of terrorism in Indonesia's violent history, killing 202 people—24 of them British—and injuring 209.

The local hospital could not cope with this massacre of the unknown and the innocent. Many of the seriously injured were lowered into hotel swimming pools in an attempt to ease the agony of their burns. Others were flown to hospitals in Darwin and Perth.

The second bomber—who had only just learned to drive in a straight line—managed to reach the Sari Club opposite Paddy's with a bomb weighing well over a ton. The third bomb, comparatively small, was packed with human excrement and detonated outside the US Consulate in Denpasar.

I went to pay my respects to the victims at their memorial on the site of Paddy's. Today, town life has returned and bustles around that unhappy corner, where visitors stop to read the long list of international names on the wall. With 88 Australian dead, their government did not ask Indonesia to refrain from using its death penalty, though not all the bombers have yet been punished.

Bali is one of the 3,000 islands of the Indonesian archipelago. A French research team from the World Bank studying this underdeveloped area some years ago presented the government with a remarkable development plan: they wanted the southern peninsula cut off from the rest of the island and turned into a £60 million complex of hotels and shops—a vast holiday camp. Contact should not be encouraged between Balinese and tourists, they said—but restricted. The islanders, the dancers, musicians and artists would be fed into these confines at regular intervals, just to entertain.

Then, the experts believed, the majority of holidaymakers would never leave their area, sparing defenceless villages the invasion by coachloads of foreign sightseers spraying these unprotected people with insensitive cameras and currencies. Much of this has come to pass.

Balinese still keep their delightful ability to mix modernity with tradition: statues of demon-giants at crossroads ward off evil spirits which cause accidents, and must be pacified by small offerings. I always worry that stopping my car at a busy crossroads to leave an offering might *cause* an accident—but that's for the relevant demon-giant to worry about.

With their happy blended lifestyle, Balinese are little touched by progress. Within villages children are revered. Infants are not permitted to touch the impure earth, for the smaller the child the nearer her soul to heaven and the purer her spirit.

In this oasis of undying ceremony, there is a collective obligation to make things beautiful. Every new event must receive a priest's blessing.

Simultaneous entertainment's provided by a puppeteer with his cut-outs, backed by the inevitable gamelan orchestra.

Though Indonesia's Muslim, this island is Hindu, mixed with its original nature-worship. In no other place is religion so interwoven in daily life—and in no other place is it such a happy, natural, smiling thing . . . I attended a marriage ceremony that was also the celebration of a baby son's first steps upon the impure earth. The fact that the boy is now 14 merely indicated that the family needed time to gather its celebration money together.

Not all is perfect in Paradise, of course. Many of Bali's 2½ million people are undernourished; four out of five live in primitive villages and must spend their days working in the rice paddies for the good of the village-commune. Their climate can be unkind—an equatorial isle sweltering under a scorching sun or, when the monsoons come, almost drowning.

Villagers must use their local river for bathing, washing clothes, watering animals and drinking. The same river can also be their crossroads and lavatory . . .

On my first visit, back in 1972, I wanted to talk to Walter Follé, a German commercial artist who was passing through on his way to Australia. Quite quickly, he married a lovely low-caste Balinese girl aged 13 and said to be the island's prettiest. She had a cigarette-stall by the roadside, and you know how it is—you get talking . . .

The monsoon certainly complicates life for visitors on this island. Should people invite you to drop in, they *mean* it. I had to wade across.

The life of Walter Follé and Madé Lunas seemed

rather like a tropical soap opera. By the time I reached the compound where he lived with his new wife and her family, it was almost nightfall. The man from Düsseldorf was sitting with his Madé Lunas outside their hut. Walter, 33 and a Lutheran, now lived like any low-caste Balinese . . . He'd left his first wife, a Hamburg model, to work in Australia, but *en route* was captured by the spell of the island—and its cigarette-girls.

I wondered how he communicated with his appealing new bride, since they had no language in common. He explained: 'She reads thoughts from my eyes.' This was ecstatically romantic, but may not have much helped communication.

Their first child, Ratna, was born the day after our interview in that '72 monsoon, when Madé was 13 or so. They ran a hotel in Ubud for a while, but Walter was not quite the white knight he had seemed. He quarrelled with the other villagers and they hated him. He left his wife with a second child when Ratna was 7. Apparently Madé was no longer 'reading the same thoughts from my eyes'!

Walter never had a Balinese residential permit so when regulations caught up with him he was finally expelled, though he managed to sneak back now and then to see his children. He settled in Australia, married a local girl and started another family. Eventually he returned to Bali where in 2004, aged 65, he died.

Madé Lunas had stayed in touch with Walter and it seems never wanted to divorce him. Recalling his active sex life, she says tolerantly, 'He couldn't help himself, he was so attractive the girls chased him.' He left her with nothing. However, she married again—a most curious man, a sort of village shaman who started having sex with her daughter Ratna when she was a child. Madé refused to leave him, so Ratna ran away and lived with her grandmother. When she returned her religious stepfather had burned all her clothes and books.

She had always idolized her father, who reappeared in her life when she was 13. To escape her family situation Ratna married at 16, started a batik shop and had a couple of children. She then divorced her husband. This, under Balinese law, meant that he took her children, her house and her shop at a time when she was also partially supporting Walter.

By Balinese standards, her shop was successful and stylish. After Walter's death, she married someone that *he* had liked. She still hero-worshipped him, though—like most of the cast of this Balinese drama—he seems to have been given more than he gave.

On the Balinese stage life's an endless pageant. Theatre is a religious offering, as is food exquisitely assembled for some divine feast. A temple dance offers the motions of daily life made exciting and beautiful as a gift to visiting deities.

The whole island's one vast artists' colony. Every Balinese is a dancer or painter, sculptor or musician; all are natural actors. The audience knows every step and word of the drama, yet they watch—transfixed—as evil is vanquished, traditionally, by the guardian of Good. A mythical animal called the Barong is always victorious.

Unlike the people of other tropical lands, the Balinese enjoy a culture so complex and sophisticated that visitors can seem awkward. This is no innocent Paradise surrendering virtue at the wave of a seductive traveller's cheque. These people believe, quite simply, that their island is the centre of the universe, and know that Bali, their Last Paradise, is still far closer to yesterday . . . than tomorrow.

16

ALL THE TIME YOU HAVE A SENSE OF IMPENDING DISASTER

'All the time you have a sense of impending disaster,' said Eleanor Alliston, talking about living on an island in the path of the Roaring Forties where she and husband John had been the only inhabitants for thirty-six years. She seemed totally indifferent to the menacing prospect it threatened.

She was small and bouncy; he handsome and quiet. John was Commander Alliston DSO, DSC and Bar, who finished the war commanding the Australian destroyer *Warramunga*. He had seen action in the Pacific, the Far East and the Mediterranean, earning his impressive accolades, and surviving—though wounded.

You needed a taxi to reach the Allistons' threatened home—an *air* taxi, from Smithton on the north coast of Tasmania. On close inspection our aircraft seemed held together by sticky tape. However, it absorbed all the punishment the Bass Strait could throw at us before reaching Three Hummock Island in thirty-five minutes and landing on a long silver beach. The entire population—both of them—came out to greet us as we bounced along the sand. John and Eleanor were welcoming—they didn't have *too* many guests—and they were after our newspaper!

When John had left his destroyer and the Royal Navy, they returned to Australia and New Zealand, looking for the right kind of living space for a brand-new family. Somewhere along the 40th Parallel, where the climate was friendly. They thought about Chile, then Tasmania, and finally reached deserted Three Hummock Island and its 23,000 acres. They bought the island's lease in 1949 and lived there for the rest of their lives, collecting impending disasters, but surviving.

Each day Eleanor would prowl around their island barefooted, dictating Mills & Boon novels into her recorder under the *nom de plume* of Minka Jones, in which girls called Tiffany and men called Rhett lived in mild conflict in some sophisticated city of the mind. Despite all her imagination, their fictitious lives seemed to me far less romantic than the *true* love story of Eleanor and John.

Meanwhile John trained his vegetables and tinkered with his tractor. They had finally sold all their cattle and sheep and, for the first time in their lives, were out of debt with no more hostile auction-rings to face. They felt liberated.

Three Hummock Island is 35 square miles of not very much. With little money and no support the Allistons struggled to raise and send out into the world four children and fourteen grandchildren. For the last ten years they had been alone again— and at their happiest, living their blend of bliss and anguish.

When I reached them in '87 they were both nearing 80 and clung to their island like survivalists: optimistic, staunch and happier than any two people I have met.

We walked the few yards from the beach to their home. It looked like a weary cricket pavilion which had sagged a bit, having stood up to the Roaring Forties for too many years. This was where Commander Alliston brought his pretty young bride from Titchfield, to start a family away from war-ravaged Europe. He carried her from their Hampshire manor house, selling the car, their silver and crystal, even the gold cocktail shaker, and after a big farewell from the cook, gardener, nanny and the Obliger, they set sail for a new life in the unknown.

They had been taken by Three Hummock Island off the windswept north coast of Tasmania—and not just by its price of 6d an acre, but by the stark appeal of this deserted island without *one* essential service. With thirty empty beaches, lagoons, rivers and valleys, the island had a natural charm. Kangaroos, parrots, peacocks and all manner of wildlife lived undisturbed in its tiny wilderness. Venomous snakes were ignored; the only animals at risk were possums who dared to eat John's carefully tended vegetables, and sometimes paid the price.

Idealistic and in many ways ahead of their time, they believed in conservation, deplored food additives, and were determined to bring up their children safely. Their nearest neighbour, shop or doctor was 40 miles away across ferocious seas. This drawback they discovered only days after

128

their arrival when their baby son Warwick, aged seven months, became dangerously ill one night. They only managed to attract the attention of a passing boat which could rescue them all by lighting three signal flares and setting fire to a derelict boat on the beach.

The baby recovered—but only just. His parents had discovered they needed more than carefree good luck to survive in the wilderness.

After the cosseted naval life of a captain of all he surveyed, John left the Navy and had to learn, for example, how to kill and dress a sheep for dinner, how to manage on a tiny budget without a fridge where food and post would arrive sporadically, dropped off by a friendly local pilot—who then complicated their lives by losing his licence.

To provide more cash and keep themselves afloat, John would spend the occasional six months in the Merchant Navy, sailing as first mate. He said it was a millionaire's life, without a millionaire's money.

They were a handsome couple, she delightfully girlish at 75 and he a little older but full of energy. I wondered whether, after all these years of living together in solitude, there was anything left to discuss. Eleanor threw back her head to laugh. 'What a lovely question!' There was *always* something new to discover, she explained.

Upon moving in, John was entranced. Eleanor, viewing her living quarters for the first time and finding two rotting wallaby carcasses hanging from their bedroom ceiling, was less enthusiastic.

Eleanor had no fear of death. Her perfect ending, she believed, would be to die with John as their little aircraft crashed, and she would be holding his hand and thanking him for their wonderful life together. Alternatively, if she died on the island she fully expected John to put her body on the compost heap to nourish his tomatoes. She had lived too long on Three Hummock to let anything go to waste.

John told me of his relief at selling the stock and being debt-free. The island had eaten up every penny they made, yet he was a contented man. He bought a tractor, and a typewriter for Eleanor— their first 'luxuries' after the auction. They still had no refrigerator.

On their rare trips to the mainland she adored ordering from room service, especially ice cream. When I asked if there was anything at all that she wanted, she did not hesitate: 'A great big square-cut emerald ring.' Sadly she never achieved that ambition, which would have suited her so.

She was still a determined dreamer with a practical nature. She rarely bothered to wind a clock or do much housework. He, dogged and honourable, had always had trouble selling his cattle at auction because the local farmers knew that, having brought his stock to market, he could not afford to charter the boat again to take them back to Three Hummock if they did not sell, so they could screw poor John into the ground while performing as traditional mates and cobbers.

I've never felt the same about farmers after seeing the stricken face of their war hero when his good Aussie neighbours ganged up against him.

At the other end of the scale there was the Tasmanian government, which would not let him buy the land he had worked for thirty-six years to hand over to his children. It was a rented paradise and they were still only guardians.

After three days on their island we waved our sorrowful goodbyes and climbed into our wobbly air taxi. I left my camera crew to collect back-up shots on the beach as we flew back to Smithton.

The Allistons waved us off their beach, and watched us leave. John turned to Eleanor. 'Well, that was *lovely*,' he said. They were his last words about us, and console me to this day.

The letters I received from Tasmania suddenly changed from Eleanor's handwriting to John's. He told me that his brave little wife was now suffering from Alzheimer's. In his 90s, and in his final letter, he told me that that Eleanor could no longer speak, 'but she smiles at me, and squeezes my hand'.

Eleanor died in 2003, John less than a year later. It was fitting that they should have got together again so quickly. To return the compliment: a *lovely* couple.

17

I'VE ALWAYS WISHED
I HAD A BETTER PERSONALITY

He looked doleful, even at happy times. I'd never seen him smile, but once or twice ran into an almost silent guffaw. Even that didn't seem happy enough, yet at the end of the day it was as close to a smile as I was going to get. He *had* to be happy now and then, surely, because . . . he was the Richest Man in the World! He was now a recluse, about whom little was known. This was about to change. Before *Whicker's World* had finished with him he had 25,000 letters in one day.

I had met J. Paul Getty socially a few times, and been invited to his Sunday lunches at Sutton Place. After living in suites in the George V in Paris and the Ritz in Piccadilly, Getty had bought a Tudor mansion in Surrey once owned by Henry VIII from the Duke of Sutherland for a laughable £65,000. This was in the early Sixties and even then he kept talking about going home to America, but he was not much of a traveller. After being caught in a tornado some twenty years earlier, he refused ever to fly again, and was equally fearful of the sea. This made returning to California something of a problem.

That Sunday he was as usual a thoughtful host, with the help of his butler Bullemore. He preferred to listen, and his rare conversational contributions were hesitant. Amid an almost overpowering display of silver our lunch was elegant, but Spartan. Getty was no trencherman. He dutifully chewed each mouthful thirty-three times—and counting—but, as with much else, didn't seem to extract any *pleasure* out of it.

He confessed to me one culinary weakness which did not put his chef under too much pressure: buckwheat pancakes with maple syrup, and cornbread. He also admitted to a lifelong enthusiasm for ice cream, and I instantly warmed to him when he confessed he had once tackled three maple nut sundaes in a row . . . That guilty excess produced the first dry chuckle of the day.

As I drove back to London that evening, I thought I had detected within our shy host, then approaching his 70th birthday, the faint but unspoken desire for a public nod in his direction—some small acknowledgement of a remarkable career. The fact that he was little known was his own wish, but now perhaps it was time to ease up on those total-privacy instructions.

The next day I put before Getty the idea that he should be the subject of the first in-depth *Whicker's World*. After some reflection, he agreed.

He was certainly a regular and informed viewer of my programmes, and had made some thoughtful and instructive comments. I confided my feelings to a wise mutual friend at the lunch, the actress Edana Romney. She had picked up the same vibes. It was time to offer television a giant leap forward.

Then I had to find out a lot more about our solitary billionaire. The precise extent of his wealth was difficult to compute—probably around $4 billion. Asked to estimate, Paul said reluctantly, 'I would hope to realize several billions.' He then added a typical Getty get-out clause: 'But remember, a billion dollars isn't worth what it used to be.'

His baptism of fire with me on television was a total success and Paul emerged as a winner of the sympathy vote. He was delighted. 'In every film there's a hero and a villain,' he told me, 'and *you* were the villain.' Certainly in America, where television critics at that time were not used to the direct approach, and some viewers thought I had been too hard on a favourite son.

His wealth could only be calculated with difficulty to the nearest million pounds, and still sounded like the mileage to Mars, yet as a three-

133

dimensional man of likes and dislikes, qualities and defects, he was little known. No key to his confusing character had been found. He was an absolute monarch. No directors or shareholders influenced his lonely decisions. The international empire controlled from Sutton Place in his 700 acres of Surrey was then linked to the Guildford Exchange by just *two* lines . . .

The condition of the poor has inspired literature, sociological investigation, government White Papers; and of course that large group is not difficult to join. Almost every one of us belongs to it, temporarily or permanently. The condition of the *rich,* however, has been generally ignored by serious investigators. It was as though millionaires were the skeletons in our capitalist cupboard, viewed only with shame and envy.

Anyone who wants to discover what the rich-rich are really like will find little reference material outside the pages of the glossies (where they generally appear fatuous) and the chit-chat of columnists (marital upsets and silly scandal).

Research in the BBC Library produced a meagre haul on Getty. Indeed, after the programme had been transmitted we had a call from *The Guinness Book of Records*, eager to add to its factual collection.

Everything about mega-millionaires is so contrary to ordinary experience that they can seem extraterrestrial. For some their very existence is an affront. For others the only objection is that their countless pleasures cannot be shared. The envy syndrome is pervasive.

Though they suffer no restriction of choice, in reality even multi-millionaires soon reach the

RIGHT: Cairo's Anglo-American Hospital, where I first saw the light …

LEFT: My first television interview for *Tonight* in front of a blitzed building with a Ramsgate landlady.

BELOW: *Whicker's World* decorating the tarmac at Heathrow.

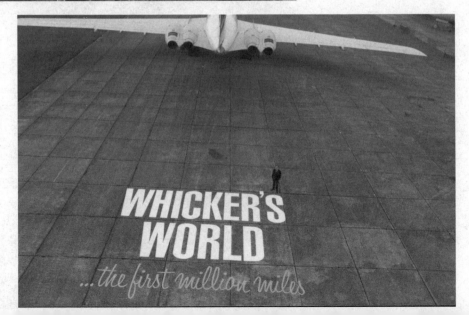

WHICKER'S WORLD

…the first million miles

ABOVE: I interviewed Harold Robbins, self-appointed 'World's Best Writer', aboard his yacht at Cannes.

BELOW: Leslie Bricusse (left) with Valerie (middle) and Evie Bricusse (right) on our terrace at Cap Ferrat.

Liza Minelli (left) and Evie Bricusse (right) had just swum ashore from their Riva, through a mistral.

Papa Doc goes Christmas shopping with daughter Di-Di.

Papa Doc attracts cheers by handing out wads of banknotes from his bulletproof Mercedes 600.

Face to face with Papa Doc and Madame Rosalee Adolph, leader of his murderous Tontons Macoutes.

Every husband needs a helpful shove—Fanny Cradock puts Johnnie in his place, for lunch.

Kathy Wagner, wife of cosmetic surgeon Kurt, stimulated our largest-ever postbag.

Their interests were different, but Kathy was his perfect patient.

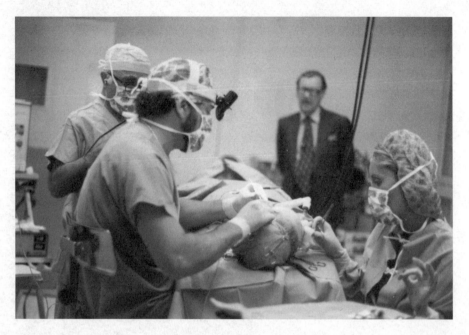

Here Kurt has just broken a grateful patient's nose, while I hold on to the furniture.

Thirty years and several procedures later, Kurt and Kathy in Boca Raton, Florida.

Midsummer in Jersey.

Valerie has words with someone her own size ...

... while another local, though better dressed, ignores the street sign.

Edana Romney, most loyal of friends, solved everyone's problems except her own.

One can coax even extinct equipment into life in a flying office.

LEFT: Dick Hughes, leader and most combative of the 'Hatmen', flew to London to support me on *This Is Your Life*.

RIGHT: Houston: Wild West meets new West.

A pride of moustaches by the Alan Whicker Appreciation
Society. Their moustaches were all darker than mine. I
pretended not to notice.

My most valued support is from old friends. (Left to right)
Jack Gold and Brian Tuffano, who've worked with me
through the years; Doug Hayward, master tailor and prince
among men; and Michael Parkinson, most generous,
cheerful and decisive of good friends.

Cecily Godfrey, fierce perfectionist and stylish iron-butterfly.

After stopping a train in Alaska, the rest of your life is an anticlimax.

On the beach at Bedarra.

Learning to
shoot to kill in
suburban Glen-
dale.

On Norfolk Island with Girlie Christian, descendant of Fletcher Christian, who led the Bounty Mutineers. One of my happiest interviews.

Every year the 2,000 islanders celebrate their ancestors' good fortune by dressing up for Norfolk Day. This scene of contentment set me hunting the globe for an island home.

Less exotic but closer to London, Jersey became our home and advocate Dick Cristin our first Jersey friend.

Lying off Sark, with Valerie.

RIGHT: Mrs Dorrie Flatman from Liverpool, a proper little madam.

FAR RIGHT: Mrs Flatman outside her main house—which is not a home …

A private paradise in Bali protected by a friendly demon-giant.

John Alliston, a brave destroyer commander, and his wife Eleanor lived their dream on an isolated island off Tasmania for 36 years.

RIGHT: J. Paul Getty, then the richest man in the world, preparing to chew each lunchtime mouthful exactly 33 times.

On Primrose Hill Brenda, the all-round villain, recalls the light and shade of a life of crime

Inspector Clouseau took Peter Sellers to Hollywood, where on a happy day I joined him for what was to be his last interview, just before his fatal heart attack.

Three times a week the silent Order of Poor Clares enjoyed 45 minutes of talk and recreation.

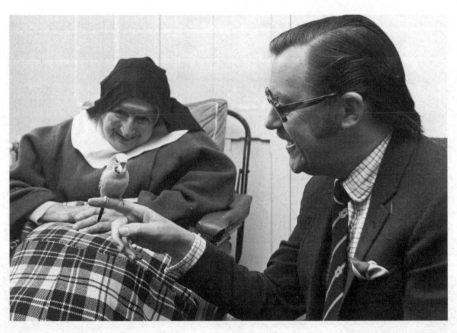

Mother John Francis entered the convent in 1896, and did not leave. She had never seen a car.

Among the Fallen in Sicily. I was one of the lucky ones.

Coober Pedy, opal capital of the world—and highly undesirable!

In Melbourne Mrs Charmian Biggs, wife of one of the Great Train Robbers, Ronnie Biggs, explaining that 'enormous piles of money have a strange fusty smell'.

LEFT: Mrs Helene Tuchbreiter of Palm Beach, known by other aspiring social princesses as Mrs Truck Driver—she was not amused.

Working with children or animals doesn't always present problems. 'Chaos' the cheetah only showed his boredom after about ten takes.

The dolphin learned how to steal my Barclaycard in *30 seconds*!

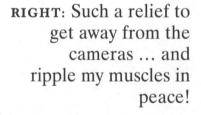

RIGHT: Such a relief to get away from the cameras ... and ripple my muscles in peace!

ABOVE: It can sometimes be easier to drive a Rolls than ride a bicycle …

Interviewing the Sultan of Brunei, a shy and pleasant man, was like having a conversation with God.

The Sultan (centre) with his younger brother, the notorious Prince Jefri (right), about to accept a polo cup from John Asprey (left) before Jefri's exile from Brunei.

The Spain you imagine but rarely capture—a private *rocio* in Andalucia.

Brunei's royal palace has 1,778 rooms and *miles* of red carpet.

ABOVE: San Francisco. In California I found some of our best stories.

LEFT: Hong Kong was my first landfall in Asia and I've been returning, always with pleasure, for almost sixty years.

Journey of a Lifetime, the *Whicker's World* team in Venice. Katherine Begg, Stan Griffin, Chris Symer and Andrew Muggleton.

A Bellini in Venice, where all the best journeys begin!

Looking out across Venice and remembering the apartment I never bought …

outer limits of purely personal gratification, which should be some satisfaction to the rest of us. They can only eat so much food, however exotic; only live in one house at a time, however splendid; only sleep in one bed, wear one suit, one watch, ride in one car, one aeroplane . . . Personal lives which from a distance glitter invitingly may upon closer inspection seem thin, brittle and unsatisfactory.

For just such a close-up inspection Getty invited me to stay within the sanctuary of Sutton Place, and subsequently film several hours of conversation. As I suspected, drawing him out proved a formidable task, for he was the antithesis of the pushy American oilman. His replies were slow and diffident—so much so that I had to snap at his heels to keep the conversation moving.

Pursuing so hesitant and morose an interviewee through the minefield of money was going in at television's deep end, for everyone's reaction to the invisible barrier of great wealth in others is intense and self-revealing. Few of us would be what we are today if we could afford to be different and, depending upon the viewers' attitude, any of my questions was going to seem naïve or censorious, deferential or aggressive.

When we talked in a businesslike way, he seemed baffled by his own staggering success: 'I really don't know of any quality I have that many others don't have. I'm hard-working, I like to think, but I know others just as hard-working. I'm intelligent, I like to think, but I know others just as intelligent— or more intelligent. I'm imaginative, but I have many friends and acquaintances just as imaginative.

'I've always wished I had a better personality,

that I could entertain people better, be a better conversationalist. I have always worried I might be a little on the dull side, as a companion.'

We deliberately put that disarming admission on the top of our programme. I was anxious viewers should not be so hostile to the richest man in the world that they would not give him a fair hearing. I need not have worried: most of them were *sorry* for him.

Hard to dislike anyone who can be so honest about himself before a television audience of many millions.

His biggest business triumph? 'I suppose just being patient, waiting for the oak tree to grow. Drilling oil-wells there's always some grief, some catastrophe. There's always what we call "a fishing job": tools lost in the hole, some unfortunate thing always seems to be happening. I made up my mind when I first started that if I carried my troubles into the bedroom with me I wouldn't sleep, so I just dismissed them. During the day I'd worry, but I wouldn't worry at night.'

He told me, quite reasonably, that he had never been interested in selling out because he would not know what to do with major money. I suggested he might just lie back and beachcomb. He liked that thought: 'I've always believed I was quite talented as an idler. Yes, if I had the opportunity to idle I could do it pretty well.'

He was wrong, of course. He had a fearful compulsion to work and enjoyed nothing more than retreating alone to his sitting room after dinner to disentangle a balance-sheet—far more enthralling than a detective story, and second only to his hidden passion: the Victorian author of

136

adventure stories for boys, G.A. Henty. They were the rosebuds of Citizen Getty. 'They take my mind off commercial things. There's not much about business or money in Henty. He's a very good example of the best type of Englishman—and that's a pretty good type.'

The solitary billionaire often retreated into that simple, clean-cut world, absorbing again and again stout volumes he kept by his bedside with titles like *Bravest of the Brave* and *Winning His Spurs*.

I asked who else he admired, and without hesitation he offered Julius Caesar, 'possibly the ablest man who ever lived'. Then Mussolini (*that* was a surprise!), Charlemagne, President Kennedy and Winston Churchill were obvious enough, but was there anyone he envied? 'I envy people who are younger, stronger and more cheerful than I am. People who have better characters than I have. There is a lot to be said for being the ordinary man in the street. Large financial responsibilities are not the key to cheerfulness.'

By coincidence CBS put out a programme in New York about a poorer millionaire, Huntington Hartford. They called it *The Reluctant Millionaire,* and their critics were not kind to him—or their profile. 'It was an unimaginative, dreary dissection of a man who turned the surface of his life over to the camera and bored the bedevil out of us in the process. It was in startling contrast to Channel 13's candid interview on Monday night with billionaire J. Paul Getty. The only question that came to mind as narrator Charles Collingwood listed Hartford's assets was "Who cares?"'

Huntington Hartford was certainly not a duller man than Getty but he had been handled differently and allowed to present his own image of himself. The Editor of *Punch,* Bernard Hollowood, reflected upon my problem: 'I have no doubt Whicker's new series of face-to-face set-to's will upset almost as many viewers as it will delight. Already I have heard people criticize his interview with J. Paul Getty as insulting and politically biased. In my view he leaned over backwards to be courteous and fair, and if we cannot ask pointed questions of a man tough enough to amass £500 million and innocent enough to believe that he is "providing work for thousands", well, the interviewing game can be written off. I hope Whicker will refuse to be dismayed and will continue to be courteous, fair and Whickerish.'

I was struggling to find some way of indicating to viewers Getty's incalculable wealth verbally, so it could more easily be grasped. I came up with, 'To be as rich as this man you'd need to win the pools every Saturday . . . for 800 years. He is several times richer than the total reserves of the sterling area. He could pay this year's income tax for every Briton—and still have millions left over . . .'

While intruding upon his private life I tried to avoid the more personal areas. Getty liked the ladies, and if he had not known much success with them it was not for want of trying. At Sutton Place I usually found an attractive companion in residence, though in the background. Sometimes two.

While we were filming it was a Rubenesque Frenchwoman who was bored to distraction by the country life where even the modest pleasures of Guildford, a few miles away, were unattainable.

I did not mention Mme Tessier or her alternates

in the programme—nor his facelift, despite those small scars behind the ears. Such facets, however revealing of character, seemed to me to be none of my business—even though Getty, to his great credit, made no stipulations about untouchable areas.

Getty was never poor, never the traditional barefoot boy selling newspapers. He and his millionaire father had decided shares were overpriced in the Twenties, so after the 1929 crash they were among the few Americans with money in the bank. They watched the market all the way down, and then bought. A lesson for us all today, no doubt.

It was a relief to learn he was not infallible. He had withdrawn from the Persian gulf in 1931 when the East Texas oil-wells came in and oil went down to 10 cents a barrel, and did not return to the Middle East until 1948. 'Had I stayed in the Gulf I would now have an industry many times greater than I have today,' he told me apologetically. I had enough trouble coping with him, the size he was.

I wondered why he concentrated his entire life upon making more and more money and he said, 'It was just to prove that you can keep in step with the regiment.' Getty had obtained a 60-year concession in Saudi Arabia for half the product of their neutral zone in which no oil had been discovered. He paid King Saud $9.4 million in cash for the concession, and agreed to pay $1 million a year for its duration, whether or not oil was struck. Four years later the Getty interests hit oil in enormous quantities, thus elevating Getty into the billionaire class, from which he never returned.

The charm of the very rich, it has been said, is the slightly hangdog look they wear. Getty certainly took his life and his pleasures with morose preoccupation and melancholy. Smiles did not come easily. I reflected that though some might think him fortunate, others would see him as a cold calculating machine. How did *he* see himself? 'As a tennis player trying to volley the ball back.' But who was serving?

'I get fifty letters a day where I'm supposed to make a financial decision. I get maybe a thousand letters a week, sometimes three or four thousand, from strangers.'

I wondered whether his wealth had made him suspicious of people, since almost everyone he met wanted something from him, and he was living in a treasure house of Old Masters. 'Well, I try not to be suspicious because that's a bad road to travel, but I find you can go into a man's house and criticize him or his wife, criticize his children, and he might still love you like a brother—but if he shows you one of his pictures and tells you it's a beautiful so-and-so and you say, "No, it's a fake," you've lost his friendship forever.'

When I reflected that lesser millionaires seemed to have much more fun and lead more satisfactory lives he recalled: 'I went to St Moritz once and my hotel suggested I give a large party. They said for prominent men it was more or less customary. I was told a certain famous millionaire had just given one for eighty people, so before I committed myself I went to see him and asked how many of his guests were friends. He said, "About five", so there were seventy-five people he had not seen

140

before. So I said I wouldn't do it—I didn't see the sense in giving a party for a lot of people I didn't know.'

We had taken pictures of the pay-phone in Getty's Sutton Place cloakroom for the use of guests who might want to make a toll call back to London, thus saving him the odd shilling. 'Right-thinking guests would consider that was a benefit,' he said firmly. 'It's rather daunting if you're visiting somewhere and have to put in a long-distance call and charge your host with it.

'You did a programme on William Randolph Hearst some time back. When I visited Hearst I was told there was one thing he did *not* like, and that was guests' phone calls on his bill. Anyone who put in a long-distance call—they went through his switchboard and they were accepted—when that person went back to his room he found his bags packed and placed outside his door.'

I doubted whether Getty would have asked Bullemore to do such a thing but . . . I was careful to keep plenty of change handy.

My own theory, the charitable one I offered when people questioned me about Getty, was that he was careful with his money because he needed to retain some nail-hold upon reality. If he did not observe little economies along with the rest of us, his money would stop meaning anything. His unlimited funds would remove him from the human race and his senses would reel before all those zeros. The solitary billionaire could not afford to lose that last touch with reality.

His fears were those of other men: disease, old age, being helpless. How would he like to be remembered? 'As a businessman—maybe a

141

footnote in history, some place.'

All his five brides spoke well of him; they included a Texas ranger's daughter, a German girl, a film starlet, a cabaret singer . . . He often expressed regret for his unsatisfactory matrimonial record, 'because I don't like any of my decisions to be unsuccessful'.

I had to put the final question: At 70 he knew, of course, that he could not take it with him. 'No—and it's probably a good thing. Might be quite a burden.' Paul Getty gave me a thin smile.

We went on to film him among his art collection, his magnificent Rubens, his Rembrandt, his collection of Veroneses, Gentileschis, Gainsboroughs, Titians, Renoirs, Gauguins, Utrillos—all of them most wisely purchased.

When we returned to Sutton Place to shoot our exteriors it had been snowing. This time we brought a helicopter and stood the uncomplaining Getty in the still white garden of his lovely home. The chopper slowly rose up into the sky above the lonely figure standing solemnly at the heart of his last home on earth. He was, as ever, the solitary billionaire.

The opinions of this unassuming man may not commend him to everyone, for the world when coldly contemplated can seem rather bleak, but they were not dangerous opinions, and indeed they may help many. Surely, I reflected, in a remote world populated by employees and strangers it was better for the rest of us that he should devote his attentions to tankers, not yachts, find his pleasures in refineries, not racecourses, paintings, not casinos.

Some time after our programme had been

transmitted, Paul sent me a note in his almost childish hand. 'Dear Alan, I enjoyed my "ordeal" very much, though I did cringe when I got a lorry-load of mail. I must say I think you treated me very fairly and handsomely indeed, and whenever you want to, you can give me as a reference. Hope you will come for lunch or tea? With cordial best wishes, Paul.'

One night he invited me to Annabel's, the elegant club in Berkeley Square. It was the last time I saw him before he died. I arrived to find among his friends at the long table he was entertaining *four* duchesses. During the lavish evening I mentioned to him that, though he did not go out much, when he *did* entertain it was in considerable style, and he gave me one of those wintry smiles. Afterwards I learned another guest had paid the bill.

Paul was being careful, right up to the very end.

Soon after completing this film I left for St Moritz for the second *Whicker's-World*-in-depth on the delightful Baroness Fiona Thyssen. Fiona and Paul had become friends, and she told me that one night he invited her for dinner at Annabel's. Since they had both starred in *Whicker's World,* they had a lot in common, and decided that they should interview *me*.

In the gloom of this sophisticated club they started working on their questions. In accordance with my mantra, that all depended on the calibre of the questions, they put their heads together and, fearful of losing their thoughts, started writing the questions down on their tablecloth.

Fiona later told me I was about to receive a going-over from experts who hitherto had always

143

been on the other side of the camera. Now I would learn how to do it.

They went for a dance to recover from their mental efforts and upon returning to their table discovered that Annabel's, with customary efficiency, had replaced their tablecloth on which they had scrawled all their best questions. Panic.

They dashed off to hunt through the club kitchens, but without success. They feared that never again would they corral such excellent questions. They finally decided they would have to start again at a later date, when they were fresh. Just before their crucial meeting, Paul died. RIP.

Years later I was passing through Beverly Hills and, since I had never seen the magnificent Getty Museum overlooking the Pacific, thought it would be a good chance on a quiet Sunday to see what they had done with all his money.

I had visited the original museum when the English director explained that their major problem was how to spend enough of the museum's incredible income . . . which was of course *Paul's* incredible income.

We were flying on next morning, so I hoped to have a look at their handywork that day. I explained to a number of significant figures at the museum that I was a friend of Paul Getty and had even debated the making of this museum with him. He was excited by the enormous museum, but had never *seen* it. It was that old hang-up about flying . . .

I even gave a museum director a couple of *Whicker's World* books showing us together as my passport to Paul's amazing bequest. They were not interested, and would not let us take a photograph. We were asked to leave.

So Paul and I were in the same position. Neither of us has seen his gift to California and the world. It's too late for Paul—and I'm watching the clock . . . !

18

THEY FEED THE PIGS ON PASSION FRUIT, THE SHEEP ON WILD PEACHES

People in the public eye are often besieged by journalists for their seasonal lists, which can save the publication a lot of editorial effort. Describe your favourite summertime menu. What would you most like to eat at a Henley riverside picnic? Explain your most comforting winter menu. Your three favourite outdoor restaurants? And so it goes.

This is a quick way for the editors involved to get a food and travel column written for them, with a little spare publicity for the victim's show or book or programme. It's free and easy, though it doesn't offer much for those ensnared. One day's demand, however, caught my attention: as a world traveller, where would you go for the best twenty-four hours of worldly meals, one dish per location?

Breakfast on the Orient Express: It is always sumptuous to greet the day from within a warm and luxurious train—so, the *Royal Scotsman* cruising around the glens at the end of May or early June. You can relax in this elegant train while

145

they move the scenery along those majestic lochs from Fort William to Mallaig, or Inverness to the Kyle of Lochalsh, in comforting slow motion. Scotland at its finest demands a thoughtful study.

Sitting in the observation car at the back with an early-morning mimosa (Buck's Fizz without the liqueur), you drift through the majesty of a scenic dreamworld, glimpsing empty motionless lochs, dark and perfect, fearful that they might vanish should you lose eye-contact even for a moment.

The *Oriental Express*, from Singapore up to Bangkok and beyond, is more spacious but of course cannot achieve the *belle époque* Mata Hari magic that has been created down the decades by the *real Orient Express*. All proper journeys start from Victoria Station, anyway. What's more, I appreciate mosaic floors in my train loos.

So, despite the competition, the perfect wake-up has to be in that granddaddy of super trains which offers *haute cuisine* and travelling magic, and is also going somewhere, purposefully, even if the cabin beds are bunks (sorry about that) and it's more comfortable if one of you waits outside in the corridor while the other dresses.

I selected breakfast while on the run down to Paris, as I did when filming *Whicker's World* on the inaugural run in 1982: smoked salmon, scrambled eggs, and their wonderful chocolate cake. So much for *my* palate.

Champagne at Saran: Leave the gleaming *Express* and drive to Épernay and the splendid château of Saran, which overlooks the vineyards where Dom Perignon was born. There, Moët et Chandon offer favoured friends lunch and dinner of such

146

magnitude that when I stayed for a week while filming their late President, the wonderful Count Robert-Jean de Vogüé, I had to keep refusing their meals—and that's unnatural.

Normal folk can only risk exposure to such rich delights for a day and a night. Anything more is too much for this world and your system. Bob de Vogüé—who drank only Scotch—organized Moët's classic champagne salute for me as we walked back to the pavilion between two long lines of sommeliers, their exploding magnums exactly controlled. He had last put on this extravagant programme for Khrushchev, who did not appreciate it half as much as it deserved. (He preferred the hard stuff that burnt the paint off his boots.)

Bellinis at Harry's: On its way to Rome, the *Orient Express* stops in Venice, where I once lived for a perfect year. Every stroll through that glorious city should end at Harry's, the first place in the world where I had an account. The bar, with the late Harry Cipriani watchful behind his cash desk, was then little known. Ernest Hemingway arrived later and made it famous. I felt most sophisticated, pushing through its swing doors, and strolling out later without the vulgar necessity of handling money. (An account merely means that you suffer one stunning blow rather than a series of unsettling shocks.)

Happily Harry's has hardly changed, though his empire—managed by son Arrigo—now stretches to America. It may not offer the best food in the world (whatever Michael Winner says!) but sitting in that crowded gossipy little bar you feel that it *does*—certainly it's the best in Venice. The waiters, who have been there forever, have the exact touch.

Brunch at Torcello: So a Bellini (spumante and white peach juice) and one or two of those moreish little *croque-monsieur* things they keep offering, and then a launch out to Torcello. Like every journey around Venice, those forty minutes across the lagoon give you an appetite for life. Pay off the boatman (if you let him wait, you'll go bankrupt) and stroll past the ladies making that lace from China, straight into Harry's Locanda for risotto, scampi with mayonnaise, and a reasonable amount of Prosecco before the regulation inspection of the Basilica.

Lunch in the Hunter: We should now be magicked to the remainder of our lunch in the Hunter Valley, a couple of hours' drive north of Sydney, at the home of my old friend Len Evans who, forty-five years ago, invented Australian wine. Sadly, the other year Len left us with only the memory of a superb and generous host in a wonderful Aussie setting, with the lovely, long-suffering Trish. Some of the most enjoyable meals of my life were spent at the long refectory table in his kitchen amid the vineyards, eating simply but very well, drinking Australian secrets—and realizing in that company how limited is my knowledge of wine.

Len had grown into a rumbustious Falstaffian figure. He sold his Rothbury Estate, though he still produced Evans Family wines from grapes around his home, still entertained fortunate friends and still, to his last day, quickly lost interest in any conversation in which he was not holding the floor. RIP.

PS: The Blue Train from Johannesburg down to

Cape Town may be wide and comfortable but, apart from the last stretch, the scenery is sad and the meals nursery.

Picnic on Norfolk Island: From Australia it's only a few hours magick-flight across the Tasman to the island that changed my life. I first found Norfolk Island in October 1960 and was instantly besotted. It is only three miles by five, a little piece of Switzerland floating in magnificent southern seas with lush grass across soft hills, valleys and around those famous pines. Here they feed the pigs on passion fruit, the sheep on wild peaches. Afterwards I went off to search the world for an island home: Capri, Western Samoa, Hong Kong, Key West, Malta, Penang, Bali, Pago Pago, Jersey . . . ?

This gentle corner of paradise, 12,000 miles from Britain and about 1,000 miles from everywhere else, was once our Devil's Island where convicts from the settlements of Van Diemen's Land and New South Wales suffered deliberate and calculated inhumanity, a place of 'extremist punishment, short of death'. Some 1,200 twice-convicted prisoners considered too dangerous to hold in Australia sailed into a regime so harsh that some blinded themselves with the sap of the milky mangrove in an attempt to escape the labour gangs, or committed further crimes to find relief in a death sentence.

The gentle peace of Norfolk which so affected me has also soothed away the torments of yesterday, placated the restless spirits of those unhappy men. It is now a place to laze and wonder—and listen . . .

> Between the soughing in the pines
> And the surging of the sea
> Hear a far-off human sigh . . .

The island was relieved of its burden of human misery in 1855, when the convicts were replaced by families of Christians and Nobbs, Mills and McCoys, Quintals and Adams—products of the most famous mutiny of the high seas when in 1787 their forefathers defied Captain Bligh and the Royal Navy to return to their Tahitian foremothers. When they outgrew Pitcairn, the *Bounty* descendants sailed on to Norfolk.

I would reach the island on Norfolk Day, which celebrates that arrival. Most of the 1,200 residents put on period costumes and go for a joyous picnic within the walls of the 17th-century prison. Scarlet tablecloths are piled with suckling pigs, great red emperor fish, tropical fruits and flowers. Their west-country accents have the low musical murmur of those who for generations have never known hurry or anxiety. 'Whataway you?' they inquire politely, in greeting. A sun-drenched Norfolk Day picnic is like no other in the world.

Heuriger in Grinzing: In the late afternoon I would fly into Vienna and head for Grinzing, for the Viennese have perfected the art of civilized drinking. They gather in the sunlit gardens of the vintners to drink the crisp young white wine, eat cold-cuts and listen to the tearful violins of wandering musicians. The whole setting is lazy, smiling and romantic—but the wine which slips down so pleasantly can have considerable after-effects.

Dinner in Puerto de Santa Maria: A few cautious

150

glasses, and on to Spain for dinner at the small castle owned by Luis Caballero in Puerto de Santa Maria, coastal town of Jerez de la Frontera, five miles away. Columbus lived here before he sailed west, hopefully.

Wherever you are fortunate enough to meet wine-makers they are hospitable, gracious and entertaining: in Épernay or the Hunter, New Zealand or the Napa Valley . . . or in those scorched lands of sherry where, amid the bodegas, centuries of British education and influence blend elegantly with noble Spanish character.

Don Mauricio Gonzalez-Gordon, Marques de Bonanza, and Miguel Valdespino joined our candle-lit table on the sandy floor of the castle bodega amid dusty rows of enormous barrels stretching into the darkness. Needless to say, we drank superbly well as three champion wine-makers outdid each other with their creations, and their charm.

Luis owned heirloom donkeys with much character, while Mauricio's bodega boasted tame mice which came down small ladders at the first scent of a dish of sherry, and got pleasantly squiffy. How can you resist?

I wondered how I could repay such hospitality: hire the Tower of London? Yes, but what about the *catering*?

Caviare at Sha'tin: For the second part of dinner I would magick major travel and allow myself to be entertained in memory by old friends in Hong Kong: Gerald and Cecily Godfrey once lived in what was the Bishop's House at Sha'tin, a tiny red structure of great elegance filled with Asian artefacts and set in a bamboo forest at the summit

151

of a tall hill, silent and isolated amid the noisy millions.

Flaming torches light the garden and play upon tropical flowers. Streams tumble into hidden pools filled with scintillating koi carp. Guests are bejewelled and Chanelled to the eyebrows: the mistress of the Ruler of Kuwait, the princess who uses the world's largest emerald as a paperweight . . . and so they go. The food *needs* to be rich.

Some of it is cooked before us in the garden on huge iron barbeques shaped like cauldrons. Then Gerald's cellar comes into play; he had the habit of sending for wine from the year of your birth or—if an unsatisfactory vintage—your conception. It's a gesture that earns a lot of face. So does the accompanying great mound of caviare, dark and gleaming and awaiting attack by mother-of-pearl spoons.

Brandy at Ephesus: Later, on board *Sea Goddess II.* There were only sixty other passengers as we sailed through the Greek islands and up the coast of Turkey. We dock in Kusadasi, go ashore after dinner and drive to Ephesus, the largest archaeological site in the world, with Roman ruins far grander than Baalbek or Pompeii. They have been taken over for the night by Cunard, for a fee of $10,000.

We were greeted by centurions with flaming torches and vestal virgins with rose petals, and led towards the Celsus Library at the heart of the ancient city on stones trodden by Alexander the Great, by Antony and Cleopatra. There we sat amid the moonlit ruins drinking champagne and listening to a string quartet. Can life get better?

Night at Jimbaran Bay: Night should be at the

152

Four Seasons on a hillside above Jimbaran Bay, in Bali. This resort has 147 villas in three villages along its terraces, each with three pavilions: one for sleeping in a great Balinese four-poster, another for disappearing into its vast Victorian porcelain bath where orchids float on soft warm water.

In the third you relax upon day-beds in front of the plunge pools, looking across its still water down to the sea, as the enchanting Balinese custodians offer a final *namaste* and disappear, smiling and silent, into the equatorial night.

19

TROUBLED SPIRITS, NEVER QUITE COMFORTABLE IN THEIR SKINS

We arrived in Jersey for ever on a calm November evening with a library of books and, in various pantechnicans, the accumulated possessions of a travelling life. In my case, almost nothing. I never collect souvenirs—but I almost collected one last parking ticket in Weymouth, waiting for the boat, until I explained what a rotten going-away present it would be.

It was the first and last time we crossed the Channel by sea—a gesture to my '64 Bentley Continental, a two-door beauty in dawn blue which always stimulates admiration. Easing our way up a deserted Trinity Hill we were growing conscious of our disadvantages in this conservative Methodist island where we knew nobody.

Though anxious to sink into our new-found peace, we were not only incomers but unmarried (shock horror), working in television (even worse) and strangers to everyone (who he?).

Leaving Cumberland Terrace in Regent's Park for a new life in Jersey was not only a wrench but a distinct change of pace for us all. I knew I was not going to miss racing up the motorway to Leeds and back every few days, spending my time in the cutting-rooms and the Queen's Hotel. Instead I would be working in my study in a new home, with the Steenbeck in one corner and in the other a brilliant view across 14 miles of sea to Normandy. That's if I was not in Machu Picchu or possibly Beirut or Barrow, Bali or Easter Island . . .

London friends had worried greatly that I might not settle in to Jersey's slower pace. There were dire warnings about a residential *femme fatale,* a pretty blonde with a taste for property developers . . . who turned out to be plump and ingratiating. Invited to a staid cocktail party at the home of someone said to be the handsomest man in Europe, I arrived with Valerie and my pretty blonde secretary Mary, who had joined us from Yorkshire. This was not wise, and created a fluttering in the Jersey dovecotes that persisted: 'Alan Whicker came with *two* girls.' Their worst suspicions were confirmed. It's doubtful that I could have organized a less suitable introduction.

Our neighbours, the Becquets, were the backbone of Jersey life. Edgar, then President of the Law Society, left each day for his chambers, dapper in a dark suit and stiff white collar. At lunchtime he would retire to the warmth of the Union Club for a game of billiards and a quick glance at the *Sun*.

Born on a farm, he remembered how French workers always spat on their hands before milking, so never drank milk. Instead he took pleasure in his home-bottled wine. He looked like Maigret, spoke with a soft Jersey-French accent and drove a racy white MGB. He was as shrewd as he was charming, and splendidly incapable of even the lightest domestic duty.

He was organized by his wife Monica, former music teacher at the Jersey College for Girls. During the Occupation she had kept the Germans in their place, and was now Chairman of Meals on Wheels and various women's organizations. She once invited me to join the intimates by addressing her as 'Sarge'. I knew this was an honour, but could never quite bring myself to presume.

They welcomed us with warmth and generosity. With them we tasted ormers, a local shellfish delicacy that required much bashing and hours of cooking, and our first Jersey bean crock. I pretended to enjoy them all, and we settled down to live contentedly on our tranquil isle, sharing their triumphs and disasters: Edgar's election to the Jersey States, Monica being knocked unconscious by a rogue apple pie which escaped from the top shelf of her freezer and laid her low with one stunning blow. Coming to, she complained bitterly at the injustice of it all: 'I only made it yesterday . . .'

She treated Edgar with a sort of resigned indulgence, his domestic hopelessness—which he made sure stayed that way—as an affectionate joke. Ringing her one morning as she returned home after visiting her daughter on the mainland, he advised her to tread carefully as a few days ago their dog had been sick on the doormat, and the evidence was still there.

The Post Office, our only shop, was run by a grumpy Jerseyman—perfect material for *Fawlty Towers*. Scattered around were elderly packets of cornflakes, assorted tins and soaps. At any moment I expected someone to say, 'Don't you know there's a war on?' Wondering one day why the postmaster wore a permanent scowl, a farming friend explained, 'Don't worry about him—we say he fancies his goat.' That sort of insult one tends to remember.

This was not, I soon discovered, the televised isle of Bergerac with a dead millionaire in every pool. The parish honorary police could easily spot a stranger on their patch. Pre- and post-war Jersey had been seen as an inexpensive place to live. It is now more expensive than the mainland, but still quiet and caring, where the Rector—ex-footballer and film enthusiast—visited his parishioners.

Many old India hands and colonial administrators settled here, plus a few ex-ambassadors. The local auction house usually offered a jumble of elephant-leg stools, Tibetan thankas and vaguely sinister African carvings, remnants of lives when there was still pink on the map.

Stepping carefully through the maze of etiquette I found a few fellow spirits. During the war I had spent time with Sidney Bernstein, founder of Granada Television, who was producing propaganda films for the Central Office of Information.

Arriving in Jersey years later I found his younger

brother Albert was ahead of me. Small and pedantic, he was married to Ruby, a rabbi's daughter with sharp intelligence and the comic timing of a music-hall star.

They lived in an unprepossessing house on the main coast road, a home chosen for its proximity to a beach they never visited, and buses they never used. Inside was a mixture of eclectic taste: a Marie Laurencin portrait, Fornasetti furniture and Picasso ceramics. They exposed their rocky landscape on Jersey's south coast to a light dusting of Hampstead intellect.

Forbidden by her father to become an actress, Ruby found her métier in public relations for Rank. Not beautiful, she carried a glamorous aura of Fifties' show biz and was one of the few women I've met who could tell a joke without revealing the punchline first.

An excellent hostess and cook, she was protected by Albert from most of life's harsh realities. Returning from a few days in London, she rang to tell him she was sitting utterly exhausted before a little quiche from Marks & Sparks. Albert, detecting she was weary, masterfully forbade her to toss the salad.

At a formal Jersey dinner her red-faced neighbour surprised her by saying, 'Mrs Bernstein, I have to tell you I think Hitler was right.' Ruby replied, 'I can give you six million reasons why he was wrong.' I never heard how he got through the next course.

There was still one topic—the Great Unmentionable—that was never discussed: Jersey's wartime sensitivities when a few Jersey girls walked out with German soldiers. Sometimes even . . . with officers. We heard stories of poor starved Russian prisoners building the underground hospital, brave young Jerseymen sailing to France or even the UK by moonlight. We saw photographs of German regiments marching past the Town Hall in St Helier, and of the joyous moment when liberation finally arrived . . . but no one ever talked about day-to-day living under Occupation. It was as though a community oath had been sworn, an agreement to leave the past behind.

Occasionally something innocent would slip out: never feeling clean because there was no soap, hiding cars beneath bales of hay, eating daffodil bulbs . . . but mostly there was silence.

Beneath the surface, memories were still fresh. I lunched one day at the Victoria Club with an amiable couple in their 50s, he a businessman, thick-set with a grey thatch typical of his Norman-French heritage, she handsome but weary. I noticed that people nodded in their direction but did not approach.

Soon after—almost before I reached home that afternoon—I was told their story, reproachfully; I should not have been sitting with them. He had been in charge of the purchase of supplies from France for the Germans in Jersey, she—a famous Olympic athlete—was 'a Jerry bag'! This was a name given to any woman who socialized, however innocently, with the enemy. There were thirty years between her lunch with the Germans and at the Victoria with us, but her story was fresh and I'm sure eventually escorted her to her grave.

My work continued: rolls of film arriving daily from the airport to be marked up for editing and sent back to YTV. Commentaries to be written and recorded.

Initially I was hesitant, even apologetic, about asking my directors to fly over to work with me, but noticed quite quickly they did not regard this as a penance: 'If anyone is coming to Jersey, it's going to be me,' said my director and old friend Fred Burnley. The only complaint was that the total absence of noise made sleep difficult for those accustomed to London; Leeds, even.

Everything was going smoothly, so we peeled off for a few days and flew down to a friend's wedding in Majorca. Returning home, I put the key in the lock—and heard the sound of running water. That is always bad news.

Halfway down the stairs to the study I saw it: a burst radiator had been spewing forth for days. Eighteen inches of water was creeping up the stairs, soaking bookshelves and, worst of all, invading the storeroom where I kept my archive: files and photographs, tapes and transcripts—the evidence of fifty years hard, in television.

If I'd not been feeling suicidal it would have seemed like one of those old parlour games: If your house caught fire, what would you save first?

We left the water gurgling maliciously and saved what we could from upper shelves: documents, pictures, files, anything we could grab and carry through the flood and up to safety. Then we laid out the sodden remnants in the garden. Papa Doc next to the woman who cared for orphan kangaroos, Palm Beach matrons with Fijian fire-walkers. As I said on camera at the time (yes, we filmed it!) it was like seeing my whole working life pass before me without having to drown—or go

159

down for the third time.

The insurance assessor was dismissive: A bunch of old VHS tapes? Worth nothing. Go and replace them at Woolworths. He saw no value in a lifetime's work that history writers may depend upon, one day.

As you know by now, I had just been asked by the BBC to look back over my fifty years of *Whicker's Worlds*, and to write this book. So what to use and what to lose? It was difficult enough, even without a flood, and it took weeks to wring out the house and wait for it to dry itself. I had forgotten how unfunny it was, dealing with insurance assessors. You certainly discover who your friends are.

We enlisted our first friend in Jersey: Dick Cristin was a clever young advocate who put the island on the financial map. It was he who brought the first merchant banks to the island and, with a few legal friends, created the island's legal/finance industry. The most talented Jerseyman of his generation, he was torn between the life he had been born into and the lifestyle he had achieved— and was not totally comfortable in either.

Our first dinner together was in a restaurant with a tiny dance floor. A band was playing loudly and exceptionally badly, drowning conversation. Dick sent them a tenner to stop playing. It was gratefully accepted—and our lifelong friendship was born.

Twice-divorced Dick lived in a house on the outskirts of St Helier, its huge rooms furnished by an over-enthusiastic friend with silk upholstery so slippery that guests sat down and slithered to the floor. He was a convivial host. Guests ranged from

Robert Plant and the Led Zeppelin mob, to any client who needed a sympathetic ear.

With a finger in many island pies, it was rumoured that his office held open house for the local police force on Friday evenings. He knew how the island worked but stood slightly apart—having chosen to make money rather than climb the long ladder of public service and social preference with a knighthood ahead. His route was rather frowned upon by Jersey-born contemporaries still awaiting their Ks.

Closest to Dick was Geoffrey Edwards, ex-miner and airman who in the Sixties had sold millions of pounds worth of arms to Saudi Arabia—mainly Meteor fighters for their air force. Geoffrey when sober was courteous and charming but believed himself to be rather dull. When drunk he was dangerous in every way—the trick was to catch him somewhere on the way up. At his home he entertained an intriguing cast of characters from Douglas Bader and the President of Barbados to various shadowy figures from the Middle East. The grounds of his manor house stretched down through thick woodland to a tiny hidden cove, like a scene from Daphne du Maurier.

Dick and Geoffrey were Jersey's Odd Couple, their adventures giving this quiet, sedate island much to talk about: Dick, caught up in the Cuban Revolution trying to buy the contents of Havana's national museum on behalf of a client, Geoffrey arm-wrestling Oliver Reed to a standstill on a Barbados beach, or holed up in Saudi Arabia without a drink for a year.

Social drinking played a large part in both their lives. Flying up to a funeral in Wales, Geoffrey

161

managed to get a pub opened at eight in the morning and, proud of his Paul Robeson voice, expressed an intention to sing 'Swing Low, Sweet Chariot' at the service. When the Rector demurred, the frustrated baritone squared up to him: 'You shiny-arsed bugger, I'll get you defrocked.' No word from the Bishop on *that* one . . .

Years later, while we were in India, he retreated to his house in Barbados, stopped eating, and simply drank himself to death. It must have been a deliberate choice—he was not happy when sober and perhaps did not like himself much when drunk. He left a pretty young wife and two small children and, drunk or sober, was seriously missed.

Our friend Dick Cristin's liver finally rebelled and gave up on him. We had watched for a couple of years as he struggled on his salt-free, alcohol-free diet, waiting for a liver transplant. It finally arrived. Months in a public ward with endless episodes of *EastEnders* had made him feel suicidal. Only nightly reverse-charge calls and visits from Professor Roger Williams, his liver guru with the beautiful wife Stephanie, kept him from giving up and going home.

His operation, one of the first of its kind to be successful, was traumatic. He hallucinated, swore ferociously at his medical team and lost a vast amount of weight. In a bleak hospital where Florence Nightingale would have felt at home he became a shrunken stick-insect with a beaky nose insisting that his food was being poisoned.

Somehow he pulled through and to our surprise became a model patient, arriving home in Jersey months earlier than expected, healthier than he

162

had been for years. He had been given a new life.

He retired from the law and became calmer, spending winters in Cape Town and acting as an ambassador for transplants, visiting patients and encouraging others about to take the dramatic step into the unknown.

I told him our home was his, though he would never be offered a drink. He went along with that, though sadly I believe he was offered social drinks elsewhere. For a few years all went well. Then, confident that his new liver could take the strain, he began to drink again.

We felt a self-righteous fury. It was as if he had no respect for the second chance that he had been given. It seemed to me a betrayal, like spitting in God's eye; but Dick had always been a troubled spirit, never quite comfortable in his skin. An addiction specialist advised us to leave well alone. An addict, however intelligent, has to make his own decisions—change cannot be imposed.

Later his beloved daughter died, the anti-rejection drugs that kept him alive attacked his immune system and illness followed illness, each more serious than the last. He survived eleven years with his new liver and finally died in his sleep, a note by his bedside asking for us to be called—so his departure was not all that unexpected . . .

20

I DON'T MIND A BEATING PROVIDED
IT'S BEDSTAKES AFTERWARDS

In 1972 Yorkshire Television asked me to do a
series about women. Germaine Greer, Betty
Friedan and the Women's Movement were yet to
make an impact, and it was still unusual to find
women in boardrooms and on flight decks.

We looked at romantic novelists with Dame
Barbara Cartland in all her pinkness, spent time
with Ivy Benson's all-women band jazzing it up in
Torquay, stood to attention with a colonel in
command of ATS learning to be soldiers at
Aldershot, and entered a convent of the enclosed
Order of Poor Clares; but perhaps our most
unexpected encounter was with Brenda, the all-
round villain, a 36-year-old career criminal.

Born to a schizophrenic single mother, Brenda
and her sisters were brought up by an alcoholic
aunt. At 10 she was caught shoplifting, and taken
into care. Her finishing school was Borstal, where
she learned the tricks of her trade, and at 15 hit
the West End, falling in with a group of
professional criminals and beginning her career as
an all-round villain. She had nine children by a
variety of men.

With plump good looks and giggly humour, she
made crime sound like an endless merry joke, and
as we walked down fashionable London streets she
explained how easy the homes were to break and
enter.

Specializing in housebreaking and shoplifting, she had also been involved with smash-and-grabs, hijacking and armed robbery, insisting that she thrived on the adrenalin-rush of the illicit act rather than the financial reward. Five spells in jail had not blunted her enthusiasm, yet somewhere within her was an unease, even a warped sense of self-righteous morality.

We filmed Brenda strolling through leafy Kensington streets as she assessed the affluent homes and explained how she worked. 'I can tell instinctively if a house is empty. They'll close all the windows, maybe leave one small one open to give the impression there's somebody in—but that doesn't fool me. If the garage is left open, if there are newspapers on the floor and letters unopened, then they're at work and I know I've got plenty of time. If there's washing on the line, she's only gone out to the shops and it's got to be done a bit lively.

'There are various methods of getting in. There's loids—celluloid—it's got to be cut to 22,000th of an inch. You run up to a little shop and tell him you want it for your scooter, then it has to be cut with rounded edges to go underneath the lock. You slide the lock back and you're in. Then there's skeleton keys, there's usually twenty-four in a set, and I know instinctively which one to use and I've got it off in a minute.

'You have to have a method. The first thing I do is put the latch down so if the owner comes back he has trouble with his keys and makes a noise. I always make sure I have a way out the back, a chair in front of the kitchen sink and the window open, just one long jump and I'm out. And of course there's always the dog element. I love dogs

165

and I make friends with them immediately. I'm always wary of Alsatians, but little yap-yaps are worse. I once had to put one of those miniature poodle things in the fridge because he wouldn't stop waking the neighbours.

'When we left, we forgot the dog! I went back to get it out even though I'd unplugged the fridge . . . It was very cold, poor thing.'

Brenda was a careful thief. She always checked for burglar alarms, being wary of those concealed in bedrooms. She liked to put things back where she found them . . . especially in the living room. But this was another ruse to confuse the householder, should he return home unexpectedly.

'You work systematically: go to the main bedroom, that's where people keep their goodies, the jewels, the furs. You find jewellery in the most peculiar places: in socks, in jumpers, even once in the hem of heavy velvet curtains.

'If the jewellery is locked up it causes a bit more aggravation, but I've got hefty shoulders on me so I can jimmy, I can use a cane. You split the woodwork and get in—you can burn through the door unless it's old English oak or some sort of impenetrable steel.

'I usually only take what I can carry and walk out of the house, so it isn't noticeable—but I have got this thing about candelabra and silver, which is ridiculous. You're not really aware of the hurt that you cause but if I get a ring with something personal written on it, or medals, I know it's personal. I make sure there's no dabs and I get them back somehow. Anyway, I'd only get peanuts for them.

'I don't expect to get nabbed but I usually wear a

wig and carry a coat of some description—some change of clothing so that if I'm spotted going in and the police are at the door I pull my wig off, put on a coat and walk out of the house so they've not seen the same person that they saw going in. I'll go in as a redhead and come out as a blonde.

'In my line of work there are men who'll urinate on the floor, ruin an expensive Persian carpet, they do diabolical things—wreck the place. I've worked with fellas like this and asked them why they do it and they don't seem to know why. It doesn't make sense to me.

'It's a bit tricky if the householder comes back. I've always been lucky, I've only come up against men, I can bluff my way out of it or I cry and say, "I'm very sorry." If it was a woman I don't know what I'd do, I might be inclined to lock her in the kitchen and forget it. I don't want to hurt a woman. I've worked with violent men and it's not pleasant, not nice, makes me realize what it's all about. I've seen violence when there's no need for violence. That brings me down.'

She was adamant that there was no honour among thieves. She'd been burgled by her own kind and felt the same pain she had inflicted upon her victims. 'I had a little flat—I'd acquired loads of goodies, and someone nicked them off me. I was very upset, just sat on the carpet and cried, and then it hit me and I suddenly thought, This is what they must feel when they come home and find their house upside down. So from then onwards I was always tidy. I wouldn't go to the police—it was obviously one of my own and perhaps their need was greater than mine at that particular time, or at least they must have thought

167

so. I didn't condemn them. I can't sit in judgement on anybody. But it didn't stop me crying.'

A professional thief will scour the newspapers for deaths, weddings and social occasions. Brenda's favourite was the *Jewish Chronicle*—not that she had anything against Jews, it was simply that they seemed to have nice furs and jewellery and she assumed that they were clever enough to be well insured, which made her feel less guilty. She was indignant about people who made inflated insurance claims. 'We've got the stuff and we know what it's worth—they should give us a few extra bob because we've done them a favour.'

She said the easiest way to access a house was to dress in shabby clothes, knock on the door and ask if there was any cleaning work available. Another ruse was to look for a house with a For Sale notice, visit the estate agent for details, then knock on the vendor's door. 'Women will ask you in, bring you a cup of tea and you get their life story. You've got to be a good listener and you've got to have good eyes because all the time you're *looking*. Then you ask to use the loo . . . and while you're finding the loo you're finding the bedrooms.'

Brenda's other speciality was shoplifting. She thought of it as the bread-and-butter of her profession, more a way of life than a profitable occupation. 'I like shoplifting, it's most rewarding, most satisfying—and I've just got to do it. Sometimes I pick things I don't particularly want and I'll give them away afterwards. I can smell store detectives—boy, can I smell them. If it's wet, they're the ones with the dry shoes, you can always tell. I tend to shoplift on my own, and I don't goto menswear shops, I'd be too noticeable, men tend to look at women.

'The stuff is easy to get rid of. The average member of the public is very inclined to buy at half price—they like a bargain. I'm not interested in clothes myself, they mean nothing to me and I only steal to order for friends. If I've made a few thousand I can lay back for a while, take a holiday, Majorca or Malaga, then across to Tangiers, somewhere I know there'll be villains, somewhere I'll find my own kind.

'I've never calculated how much money I've stolen over the years, but it's an awful lot. Once four of us went into a hotel with a jewellery section in little glass cases and we got a bracelet worth £3,000 and a necklace worth £9,000. Another time we got £2,000, and we divide it between us—it's £600 here and £900 there and it all adds up.

'I remember one time I was in Notting Hill and some friends asked me out to dinner. We were in a Jaguar and they were going to take me somewhere really nice, and we went to the end of the road and suddenly out comes the stocking masks and they say, " 'Don't worry, darling, we're just going round the corner," so off they went and they came back pulling the stockings off their faces. We went and had a marvellous meal, a cabaret and everything, and next morning I picked up the papers and they'd done a bank robbery raid and I didn't know a thing about it.'

She had little respect for the straight world. 'We did a television shop once, got straight past the lock and emptied the shop. We went back two weeks later and he'd put the same lock back on—so we emptied it again!

'Just look at an everyday man who goes to work

for his little fiddle, maybe he brings home a gallon of paint to paint his house, or some petrol. It's a perk, it's part of life. You've got to justify something because if you don't justify something, it's wrong. In the criminal fraternity, even the man who kills somebody will justify it in his own mind.'

Life did not always run smoothly. After one shoplifting spree Brenda and her friends were caught robbing a furrier. 'We'd been grassed, truly grassed by this woman who'd done a lot of bird and was wanted on a housebreaking charge so she gave us up to get off herself. Next thing I know we're on a conspiracy charge. I can remember at the time I said to her, "I hope you die screaming of cancer"—and she died of breast cancer. I find it very hard to forgive myself for that.

'We found ourselves in Number One Court at the Old Bailey with all those judges in red robes with posies of flowers in front of them, and all I could think of was Christie and Haig and the people who'd been there before me, and I thought, What am I doing here? I don't belong here. I haven't murdered anybody. We started off with twenty-six charges and were found guilty on five— I got two and a half years.

'I've been in Holloway about five times, sometimes on remand and a couple of sentences. It's so degrading, so disgusting. There are bars everywhere, it's worse than a cage. The windows are right at the top of the cell, so you can't see out unless you climb on a chair. When I was there the place was full of rats.

'They let you see your family once a month but they take away your identity. They don't let you think for yourself, they don't let you do anything for yourself. I believe you're allowed to wear your own clothes now, but when I was there the shoes were like men's boots, the stockings were thick, they gave you a skirt that was miles too big and you spent hours trying to make it fit. They called you by your last name or by number, and you had to answer Miss to everyone.

'The prison service seems to attract inadequate people. We, the prisoners, are inadequate, the people looking after us are inadequate, so it's a disaster. How can anyone enjoy locking somebody else up? Most of the women who work in prisons are bastards, prisons attract the wrong kind of women, women from broken marriages. Why does a woman want to be with another woman if she's not homosexual or if she's not got tendencies?

'I've got all the time in the world for the old screws, the ones that have been there for twenty years, because you know if you've done something wrong they are going to nick you but they're not going to lie and run to the Governor. The young ones, the keener ones, the ones we call key happy, they can't wait to get you and bang you up. One in particular, if I ever saw her I'd cheerfully run her over.

'I don't want to do bird, I find it very hard, I don't do it easy. You've got to fight, you've got to behave like an animal, and I don't want to. Apart from that I'm too old. I don't want to go away again.

'I did have one hilarious moment in the nick. Pentonville men used to be sent over to do odd jobs. They'd send over the worst-looking fellows they could find, bald-headed, eyes going in different directions, but at least they smoked and

171

you could get smokes off them. So I started to write to this one, we'd spend hours composing these gorgeous letters and he used to get me pink Camay soap out of the canteen. Then he sent me a message saying, "I'm going to cop for you," and I thought: You've got some chance, boy.

'He was working with an outside man, a maintenance man, and to my alarm the man was keeping watch. He just said to me, "Drop 'em," so I said, "Drop what?" and he said, "Your drawers, because you're going to cop." I thought, Well, if I scream I'm nicked, if I submit I might enjoy it. So I submitted gracefully.

'I dropped my drawers and I was up against the boiler that dried all the clothes and I've got my backside against it and I land up with the two biggest blisters on my backside you've ever seen. I never stopped laughing all the way through, he'd just done a six-year sentence and after he'd finished he flaked out on me and I didn't know what to do to bring him round. I was in hysterics, going mad, patting his face and everything.

'Two days later I went across to the chiropodist—and you know you get these lesbians in prison? There was no room to sit down so I sat on one of their laps and he was watching me through a keyhole. That night I got a letter from him telling me he'd sold me to one of his mates for half a crown and thought he'd got a bad deal, so that was the end of that little romance.

'Another time I was working in reception and a midget came in. She was very tiny, about three feet tall. I said to the officer in charge: "I'll bet you a nicker she's in for prostitution." And she was. We said to her, "How do you do it?" and she says,

"Well, for men I'm a novelty. I do it on dustbin lids and stand on dustbins." '

From Holloway, Brenda was sent to an open prison. At night she would squeeze through a tiny kitchen window and meet her boyfriend behind the local church, so soon she was two months pregnant, and decided to escape.

It was not the first time that she'd absconded. At 15 she had run away from Borstal, starry-eyed and impressed by the swaggering gangsters of the West End. 'Those old villains, they really had something. I was mixing with this one and that one, they were like TV personalities. My admiration for them, the Kings of the Underworld, was probably greater than for somebody on TV.

'There was a deep communal bond when I first hit the West End. They were taking bets whether I'd become a grass or whether I'd go to work and become a thief. I knew I didn't want to be a grass so the other alternative was to go thieving—and it escalated from there. You sort of go on to bigger things. As a woman you tend to want to impress. The men probably laugh at us but we want to keep up with them, at least that was the mentality I had a few years back. In fact, not only did I want to keep up with them, I wanted to go one above them, and I wanted to be friends with them, to be one of the chaps.'

Only once was she tempted to try prostitution. Her first client turned out to be her boyfriend, who beat her up and broke her jaw. She spent eight weeks in St Mary's Hospital and decided that this was not the life for her, though she had plenty of friends who were on the game.

'Prostitutes, they're nice people, so genuine.

They'll give you anything if you're skint. I've got one mate who caters for cranks, people who have fetishes. She used to have one client who wanted to be a dog; she'd put him on a lead and walk him around but she had to get rid of him because he kept passing water on the furniture and the place started to stink a bit.

'It was nothing to walk into that place and find a man chained by his genitals to the gas stove and get told to give him a kick as you walked past, because that was what he wanted. People pay hundreds of pounds for this and want you to dress up in black leather—I can't do it, but I used to go down there for a laugh.'

For all her bravado and bonhomie, there was something reflective and sad in Brenda. Most of the time she was a bawd, a Wife of Bath, then the mask would slip and another person would be revealed.

'My life may sound like a romp, but in actual fact it's not. You're either up there on cloud nine or you're very low and feeling dejected. There doesn't seem to be a happy medium. I don't want to be a villain, I don't want to hurt anybody. I try to stay away from reality, like kids out in Pakistan and things like that. Reality has never appealed to me because it seems so very nasty. Most of my time I've mixed with the criminal fraternity because, let's face it, it's a farcical world, a world of delusion, but you get to a stage when you start to question it.

'At one time I could say in all sincerity that I would do these things and have no feelings or worries. In those days I could live with myself and just not think about it. It's easier not to think, not to have a conscience, specially a guilty one.

'The excitement of getting that £2,000 is far greater than the money itself. I really believe it's a sickness, a compulsion. It's terribly hard to explain the feeling you get when you get home and see what you've got, it's almost like a sexual feeling—it's like a sexual climax. You're not aware of your heart pumping but the minute you get away the feeling of elation is something else. I don't steal for gain—not unless I'm totally skint. It's not greed, it's just my way of having a go at society and people in general.

'I regard myself as a fairly intelligent person, and I see the criminal world for what it is. It's a very high world and a very low world, low to the point where I've tried to commit suicide four times because I don't want to go on living.

'When I'm high it's wonderful, I'm invincible and nothing can happen to me, but boy, the comedown is so big, it's unbelievable—and there's no happy medium. I'm not knocking it, it's been very good to me, but I want to enter a different world now, something that provides the same excitement.

'I've reached an age where I've got a bit smarter and I want to pack it in because it makes no sense, but there's the excitement. If I'm going to pack it in I've got to find something to take the place of shoplifting that gives me an equal amount of kicks. And I'd like to contribute something now. I've done an awful lot of taking and very little contributing, so I think I should start worrying about leaving something behind that's worthwhile.

'An awful lot of people I know are violent, and I find violent people don't have much intelligence and really violent people have no intelligence at all. Who in their right mind would take pleasure in cutting someone to ribbons? It must be some sexual thrill. I've been to bed with a man who cut someone to ribbons and he was useless—I told him he was inadequate, as a man in bed.

'I've had boyfriends who've been violent—I bring out the violence in a man, I make no bones about it, I can be diabolical. I've had my nose broken twice in a fortnight, I've had my forehead hanging out, and when I told one man I wanted to leave him we were five storeys up so he opened a window and said, "You can leave out there"—he had me half way out, and I changed my mind.

'I've had so many beatings I've decided I'm a masochist. I don't mind a beating provided it's bedstakes afterwards, that's OK—I think it's like a normal woman who takes a slap from a man.

'There's loads of hidden violence in me and I'm suppressing it the whole time. It comes out occasionally and I don't like what I see. Something comes over me when I've had too much to drink and I'll end up in a fight and it's most ungainly for ladies to fight. I don't understand myself. The violence is stronger than me.'

On our last day of filming, Brenda arrived, flustered and emotional. She had come straight from court where she had watched her 19-year-old son being charged with shoplifting. She was distraught. 'When I went to court this morning I felt the total degradation of it all. I've walked in many many docks and I've never felt like this before, I just wish it could have been me in his place. I feel sick. This is his first arrest. He should take a good look at me after I've been thieving.

I'm totally and utterly exhausted, he'll realize it's not fun. If he'd been sent down I'd have gone mad. I'd have taken that court apart.

'I feel a complete failure as a mother and I feel for my husband. He's straight and works hard for a living, he's done everything in his power to bring his children up in the correct manner.

'I have a terribly guilty conscience about my children. I couldn't cope, I'd put myself in a situation where I'd go to jail to run away from my kids. I've had nine children, seven sons and two daughters, and I've lost count of the number of abortions. I sincerely hope that my children are not going to be criminals. I'm glad I've had the experiences, I've had the lot, but if I had my time over again—let's put it this way—I'd do some of it but not all of it. I never thought of the consequences but now I do, and I don't like the consequences. I don't belong in Holloway.'

She knew it would be difficult to change her life. If she stopped thieving her friends would think she had lost her nerve or become a grass—a label that horrified her. She could never become an informer, though she didn't have much confidence in her criminal colleagues. If there was a reward and money involved, there was no loyalty.

In her own mind she had a certain morality. Breaking into a house where there was a large stash of cocaine she ignored it, but finding pictures of child pornography she scooped them up and sent them to Scotland Yard in an envelope marked with the man's name and address. She was an ardent royalist and extremely patriotic, yet angry, antisocial and full of contradictions.

A few days after we finished the programme on Brenda, a curious thing happened. I was sitting at my desk in my flat and heard a noise. There in my bedroom was a well-dressed, middle-aged woman. She was not a bit disconcerted. She said, 'I'm looking for Mrs Jones,' or somesuch. I manoeuvred her to the door and pushed her out . . . I don't want all-round villains surprising me.

A few minutes later she reappeared, remonstrating with me for suspecting her motives. Had she come to retrieve something she'd hidden? Was she checking to see whether I'd called the police? I never found out.

21

THEY LIVE IN BAREFOOT POVERTY —AND NEVER SEE A MAN

After breakfast I drove up to Baddesley Clinton, between Birmingham and Warwick. The nondescript mansion had no identity—yet this is where it all began. I was feeling unsettled, worrying about the women who might greet me at the door. Some of them had not seen or spoken to a man for twenty, thirty, fifty years. One of those Franciscan nuns had lived within this enclosure for seventy-five years. Others, much younger, had only just surrendered—cut themselves off from the world. All were living in barefoot poverty and silence.

What kind of women were they, passing their

lives within a stark building they may not leave, living lives little changed since the 13th century? The most *un*liberated women in the world: the shadowed ladies of the enclosed Order of Poor Clares.

Mother John Francis had entered this convent in 1896 and since that day had never returned to the world outside, never seen a motor car. This old lady of 94 reinforced my belief that nuns live for ever. She believed seventy-five years within these convent walls had rewarded her with a full and complete life. She had no desire to see anything of the outside world, no curiosity about the life she had missed. No wonder I was worried.

Another Poor Clare, Sister Mary Francesca, writing in a pamphlet approved by the Bishop of Middlesbrough, recalled one priest's views: 'He said the vast majority of outsiders cannot see any difference between the lives of the inhabitants of Dartmoor or Wormwood Scrubs . . . and the inhabitants of enclosed monasteries.' The comparison made her somewhat indignant, yet she had to admit that Father was right about the similarities. 'The enclosured walls, the grilles in the parlour, the bolts and bars, locks and keys, the infrequent visitors . . . yes, *just* like Holloway.'

This Franciscan Order had to be understood. It was not founded to care for the sick or orphans or the aged, to lecture students or convert Aborigines, it was founded to *pray.* The nun who makes a vow of enclosure sets about praying for the millions who have neither the time nor the inclination to pray for themselves. Outside she worried about her own domestic problems. Here she surrendered freedom to bear, she believes, the

179

suffering and miseries of the whole world. Contemplative nuns are convinced they can do more for mankind, for you and for me, by living cloistered lives of poverty, chastity and obedience.

I was delighted to learn that St Clare is also World Patroness Saint of Television, so declared in 1958 by Pope Pius XII. It seems that on the eve of Christmas 1253, too ill to attend midnight mass with her community, Clare's prayers were answered. Helpless within her cell she was able to see the service and hear the friars singing in the Basilica of St Francis. On 12 August comes the feast day of St Clare, that very first viewer who was given the unique grace to follow the midnight mass from her sickbed where she remained immobile and helpless. She could see the altar and the Holy Child in the crib, she could hear the music and the singing of the friars.

The nuns of an enclosed Order may never leave their convent, never see the outside world. They live in barefoot poverty and never see a man, save only their confessor who remains in another parlour behind the bars of the wall-grille. They live in silence. Each day they pray for more than seven hours and have one vegetarian meal. By permission of the Mother Abbess relatives may visit three times a year and talk to the sisters in another room through those bars.

Each day their seven hours of public and private prayer began at midnight with the Divine Office. During the next twenty-four hours they work around the convent for six and a half hours and sleep for the same amount of time. Eating takes only forty-five minutes. On Great Penance Days the meal is eaten from the floor.

On Mondays, Tuesday and Thursdays the nuns may talk as they enjoy forty-five minutes of recreation. They never read a newspaper, hear radio, see television. Despite so consecrated a life I found these contemplative ladies delightfully jolly during their recreation. I filmed their daily routine from midnight prayer until they retired silently to their cells at 9.30 p.m.

There were then more than 12,000 Poor Clares around the world, 356 of them in eighteen houses in Britain.

Evil may be a real and tangible force but so, fortunately, is good. Around the world I have met many Papa Docs, many malevolent men—and women—so am always totally disarmed when the pendulum swings across and I stand confronted by simple and absolute goodness.

Such was the peace within the convent that among the silent sisters my Yorkshire Television crew went on tiptoes, whispering. Yet during the forty-five-minute recreation the nuns were a fun group. In that cold and spartan convent it was hard to remember that to them we must have seemed as unusual as Martians. These cloistered ladies who prayed for more hours than they slept, and lived with downcast eyes, relaxed with an unusual game of football—or even a serious session with billiard cues.

Their Order is severe. To some they are poor misguided women—even a sinister sisterhood; to others they promise the world's spiritual salvation. I asked Sister Francis if her enclosed Order really was the Church Militant, the most demanding of Orders. 'In many ways it is,' she said, 'particularly I suppose for someone like me who is very fond of meeting people and going out and things like that. The most difficult thing is getting up during the night. Even after eight years that's always a bit of a pull.'

I wondered what she most missed from the outside world. 'Not being able to feel the wind blowing all over my ears and hair. Very often you might feel absolutely lousy—excuse the word—but it's God's will that matters.'

What was the drop-out rate for novices? 'About 50 per cent,' said the Mother Abbess. 'This is like a television studio. From one place *you* reach out to everywhere in the world. We reckon we're the same. There are seven and a half hours of set prayer, but then there are periods of private prayer, quiet prayer, personal prayer . . .'

I interrupted the nuns playing hardball and asked Sister Gertrude about her calling. 'Never had any doubts,' she said. 'I've always wanted to be a nun, always, ever since I was 11. In a convent you attain perfection gradually. It was the Midnight Office that attracted me because they always say there are a lot of sins committed in the world at night-time. I wanted to give myself to God, but you can't play with fire, you cannot do two things.'

I asked Sister Veronica if she had played with fire. To my surprise she said, 'Well yes, I did a bit really, yes. I didn't always want to be a nun. It came as quite a shock to me and everyone else that I *did* want to get married. I was 22 when I came in and it was not exactly what I had in mind, but when God makes a decision it's very hard to ignore Him. He's very persistent.' Sister Veronica went on to become the Mother Abbess of Baddesley

Clinton.

Later I went on to listen in one of the parlours where Mr Sutton, a local Jaguar engineer, and Mrs Sutton were visiting their daughter Jean, now Sister Margaret Mary. This young, strapping girl had to decide whether to take her final vows next year and be lost to her parents for ever.

Mr Sutton was still undecided about the verdict. 'I think in the end she'll say, "No, I'm coming out."' Mrs Sutton said that was her husband's wishful thinking.

We were in the visitors' parlour where once a watchful guardian nun would sit listening to any visitors talking, but now there was only a token wooden grille to remind visitors of their position.

I could see Mrs Sutton was close to tears as Mr Sutton said, 'We can accept it now.' Mrs Sutton: 'We accept it because we have to, but we still wish it hadn't happened.'

Sister Margaret Mary recalled the moment when in a bookshop she picked up *The Right to Be Merry* by an American Poor Clare. 'The contemplative life had never clicked for me. Anyway I put the book down and walked out of the shop and it was as though someone said to me, "That's what I want from you." Well, I had just left the book, thinking, You must be mad.'

I reminded the young nun that although she was leading a very unselfish life, in the convent she was selfish towards her family who did *not* want her to take perpetual vows.

Sister Margaret Mary: 'This is the whole point of our life. We're doing what God wants, we hope. This is total dedication to him. I know I'll see my parents again, three times a year—or maybe more if the situation allows it.'

Mr Sutton: 'If the rules say only three visits, three times it'll have to be.' I asked Mrs Sutton if that was enough. There was a long pause while she fought back her tears, and finally offered a soft, quavering 'Yes . . .'

We filmed this agonizing scene some forty years ago, but I have never forgotten poor Mrs Sutton's stricken look as she realized she had lost her daughter.

At the end of our filming, when we left the Poor Clares to their holy lives, we wanted to leave them some token of our visit. This was not easy because, with such vows of poverty, any gift would instantly be passed on to the poor. Then we remembered they had told us that much of their garden produce went stale, so we bought them the biggest deep-freeze we could find. It was almost too heavy to move. As we drove away for ever, a gaggle of excited nuns came out to manhandle it towards their kitchen.

They sent me an illuminated blessing from St Clare, Patroness Saint of Television. It has been on my study wall ever since. I'm happy to say she still seems to be taking good care of me.

22

A FEW LEFT BEHIND
WHEN THE TIDE RAN OUT

All round the world I run into characters left
behind when the tide went out. I reached
Cooktown in Northern Queensland, halfway up
Cape York, in 1961 before their wonderful
Australian Outback became a film set. It then
seemed as though only one Brit had got as far
north as this and he, I discovered, had been a
floorwalker (as they used to call that role) in
Harrods. He was now a jettywalker doing a spot of
gentle fishing when I disturbed him. It was *Are You
Being Served?* in the northern Queensland
Outback and seemed to me the perfect escape, for
the Coral Sea was gentle, the sun glorious, the
people absent.

Some of my beachcombers had dropped anchor
where there was no beach. Some were still holding
on to an echo long gone. Others had just found
themselves mislaid, somehow, and without the
means or energy to get back to that tedious job in
Surrey. They usually wanted to join the others
but—you know how it is—found that everybody
else had gone on without them, so made the best
of things as they were.

Some thirty years ago when I was filming a
second series in Australia, I interviewed Charmian,
the wife abandoned by the Great Train Robber
Ronnie Biggs when he fled to Brazil. There was
also that American master-forger in Sydney who

had difficulty spending all his banknotes. There was Prince Leonard of the Hutt River Province and many others—all strong memories about extreme people who had somehow taken a different turning.

So for a townful of them we decided to look at Coober Pedy, a mining town some 500 miles north of Adelaide which produces most of the world's supply of opals. We flew in a tiny plane to a sandy strip in the middle of a bleak desert where heat sucked the air from your lungs.

The climate was so fierce that 80 per cent of the population choose to live in dugouts below ground, modelled on First World War trenches. Here at least the temperature stays a stable 75 degrees, and fly-free.

With forty-five different nationalities in a population of 3,500, Coober is one of the strangest inhabited places on earth—or under it. Like turning the clock back to the days of the gold rush, miners work in hideous conditions and dream of striking lucky. Frequently at night there was gunfire, followed by the arrival of the Flying Doctor: Serbs and Croats taking pot shots at each other? Prospectors trying to steal each other's finds? Family feuds? All frontier life was there ready for the digging, or the stealing.

By day everything was covered in a fine red dust the colour of baked beans. Each evening I would strip off, put my clothes in the shower and stamp on them as red liquid oozed away, like a scene from *Psycho*. Bathing was also hit-and-miss; in our basic living quarters water would stop abruptly if someone with a better plumber turned on a tap.

The three-day drive by road from Adelaide

meant that goods in the lone shop were scarce and luxuries non-existent. The General Store sold everything from food and clothing to spades and explosives, so was at the centre of life. Antonio, the proprietor, was a middle-aged Italian who, finding he needed more help in his shop, had gone back to his Sicilian village in search of a wife. He returned a few months later with a young bride. Much excitement—though there was something they all knew, but she . . . did not.

Nothing could have prepared this girl for life in Coober Pedy with a man she hardly knew—and now did not want. Away from her family, parted from everything familiar and transplanted to an isolated, scorching dot on the edge of civilization, she was completely alone. Worse was to come. She was the last in town to know that her new husband . . . was gay. The local Aborigines, sensing her unhappiness, gave her an orphaned kangaroo to look after. It died. She was bereft.

When we rolled into town—fresh faces from the outside world—she clung to us instantly as misplaced Europeans, following our footsteps everywhere as we explored this weird place. What could we do for her? We could not take her with us, yet hated the thought of leaving her scorched and withering away.

As days passed news came through that some sort of airport strike was imminent. The little five-seater single-engine plane that had delivered us was about to be cancelled. Hastily we gathered our gear and headed for the airstrip to grab the last means of escape—an enforced vacation in Coober Pedy was not inviting. There she was, by the plane, watching as we raced past her towards freedom.

'Maybe you'll come back here for a holiday,' she said softly, imagining the most impossible happening.

I'll never forget that wistful little face.

Others choose to stay washed up on foreign shores, flotsam of another age. Sjovald Cunyngham-Brown, born in the Shetlands, had been the last British Governor of Penang. After independence he chose to be absorbed into the island's post-colonial melting-pot, far away from the Somerset Maugham style of imperial Malaya. In his late 70s, he now lived far from the grandeur of Government House, with an esoteric collection of Oriental artefacts and an enthusiastic appetite for his favourite tipple: nourishing Martinis.

In the Thirties, long before Buddhism became fashionable in the West and hippies embraced Eastern meditation, Sjovald had discovered his own brand of mysticism from an old Rajput aristocrat. Hard to imagine what the senior administrators made of this young man who had, in their eyes, gone native. During the war he was quickly captured by the Japanese and spent years imprisoned in a dank dungeon in Sumatra.

In his cell he practised what he had learned, concentrating on creating in his mind the image of a rose. So strong was this image that he could feel it—even smell it. Another prisoner passing his quarters demanded, 'Where did you get that soap?'

Of the 3,800 prisoners in the camp only 800 were still alive when liberation finally arrived. Sjovald survived the ordeal by faith—and by eating the only protein available: insects. He was convinced that many prisoners died unnecessarily because they were too squeamish to follow his example.

Emaciated and naked, he was liberated by an impeccably dressed Lady Edwina Mountbatten. Sweeping in on the first Allied plane to land on the bombed-out airfield, she flicked open her gold cigarette case and offered him a cigarette; within hours he was bathed, dressed and smoking a cigar in the Residency at Johore. He said it was the strangest day of his life.

Also near Penang in the Seventies was Dr Reid Tweedie, a doctor of the oldest school and a true remnant of the Raj. He believed that the downfall of Empire, the loss of India and subsequent loss of British face, were all due to Clement Attlee who was seen struggling to remove his shoes at the gates of a Hindu temple. Thus was his image ruined. He himself had not taken his own shoes off, he said, for forty-five years. He would clap his hands and servants would appear from all sides and do the job for him.

His surgery beside a rubber plantation was a small dusty room with barred windows and various coloured liquids in glass containers on a window sill, untouched by any medical advance in the last fifty years. His speciality vitamin treatment was administered by the sort of syringe normally used to subdue elephants.

He believed that anything less antiquated than thick reusable needles would have a detrimental psychological effect on his patients. With Dr Tweedie's noticeable needles, each patient knew that he'd got his money's worth.

He was driven around in a large air-conditioned car wearing a sola topi and wrapped in several layers of sweaters—he was ever fearful of catching cold in such tropical heat. A believer in the redeeming qualities of whisky and antibiotics at the merest hint of a sore throat, he was oblivious to the modern medical world. Dining with him after our conversation he proudly introduced his cook, insisting that she made the best mashed potato in Malaysia. This may have been the case, but unfortunately the fluffy white mound was crawling with ants. Our strict dietary apologies had to be explained.

Today this eccentric old Scot would have been branded a racist, I would have been criticized for not attacking him . . . and fifty years of irascible but effective medicine among the plantations would have been lost.

In Paraguay, making a programme about the dictator, President Stroessner, I borrowed a secretary-interpreter from a friendly bank manager. Anne was a priceless asset, warning of the dangers all around; the pyragues, the General's 'people with hairy feet', who spied upon suspicious gringos like me. Blonde and statuesque, Anne would have turned heads anywhere, but here in Asunción among small, dark, native Paraguayans she was a sensation. Cars stopped, whole streets fell silent.

As usual with such wanderers, her story was unusual. She had been a typist in Notting Hill but was desperate to learn, of all things, how to play the national instrument of Paraguay, the harp. She saved and set off, reaching Guyana where her money ran out. Forced to break her journey, she went up-country, earning her living by capturing animals for zoos.

She married the man who owned the shack-hotel

in the jungle village where she had been staying, had his child, divorced him and finally reached Asunción with their son. By the time we met she had attained her dream; she was an impregnable harpist, from Notting Hill.

23

NO MONEY, NO ENGLISH— AND NO TROUSERS

I've always believed that within each of us there's a great television programme, a secret interview ready for headlines. All you need to do is nod sympathetically—and out comes your revelation. So it was that today's surprising revelation would be *Whicker's World* attempting to keep two programmes safe within the BBC schedules, and not defecting to ITV. It all sounded rather unlikely.

At that time a popular series on BBC TV was *Come Dancing*—a simplification of the *Strictly* which appeared some forty-five years later. How life doesn't change.

The BBC's agreement with Mecca Ballrooms was then due for renewal, and they were anxious to talk—but newly rich Independent Television was dangling large offers before the entertainment octopus of Mecca, urging it to dance across to commercial.

The head of the BBC department responsible for such entertainment was Peter Dimmock, who came on to me in a high old panic to say that the man he was in negotiation with was Mecca's joint Chairman, Carl Heimann, who had just seen my Paul Getty programme and longed to be the subject in a similar project, for his private viewing.

New thought. I was not used to being *asked* to dance—for an audience of one, what's more—so was unenthusiastic.

Mecca at that moment also owned *Miss World*—another hot property—so Dimmock was desperate to keep him sweet and begged me at least to go along and talk to Heimann, just to show willing. I was not much interested. The whole exercise seemed to be some businessman's desire for instant glorification. However, for the sake of Our Side I agreed and on my way home that night called at a small house near Exhibition Road, Kensington, where a precise little man told me his extraordinary story:

Carl Heimann had taken his first job at the age of 13 as a commis waiter, a piccolo, in his native Copenhagen. For three shillings a week he worked from eight in the morning until midnight, with an hour off at midday. Not unreasonably, he decided to escape to America, but found it would take months to raise the fare. By 1912 he had saved just enough to get part of the way—to England.

'If you travelled steerage you had to show £5 in cash when you arrived,' he told me, 'which I had not got. If you travelled first class you didn't have to show any money. They assumed you were affluent. After paying that fare I had exactly 27 shillings and the address of a lodging house in Charlotte Street. They charged a shilling a bed for a night, and in the room I was allocated I found there were already three other people: a man, and a couple in the double bed. I was too tired to care.

'When I awoke next morning they had all gone—and so had my 27 shillings, *and* my trousers. On my first day in London, aged 16 and unable to speak a word of English, I had no money—and no trousers.'

From that daunting introduction, Carl went on to become a multimillionaire controlling a nationwide organization of 8,000 employees providing Britain with much of its indoor entertainment. He ran fifty-two ballrooms, seventy bingo halls, six ice rinks, forty restaurants, and he catered to much of the State's recreation—from the Arsenal and Tottenham Hotspurs cafés to the Ministry of Defence luncheon club and the Cabinet Office canteen.

Carl Heimann believed in himself. He was 70, and had just been married for the second time, to Brownie—a most attractive partner. Rather to his surprise, they had a son, Stuart. Between his two children there was a gap of forty years. He had also suffered his first heart attack, feared for his second, and wanted to leave some pictorial memories for his boy, then aged 2 . . .

His anxiety got straight through to me—the one television man he could have approached to film his story who also had no memory of his father because of his untimely death. Carl explained why he wanted to be interviewed and, it seemed to me, his sensible and significant idea. He hoped to leave his son a walking, talking private memorial so that one day the boy could say, 'That's my dad.' I wonder why more people don't do that.

I agreed at once that my own company would produce a film for Stuart, and I would interview his father. It occurred to me that I ought to move into the obituary business and call my company *Immortality Inc.*

So we filmed a lot of conversations, and I observed Carl presiding over a number of his pink-and-gilt establishments: the Empire Ballroom in Leicester Square, the Café de Paris, Hammersmith Palais, various Locarnos and Lyceums . . . where I was learning about his survival on a few pennies' worth of chips when he walked to Southampton, begging meals along the way, and became a steward on a liner. So he worked and starved towards his first business: a café in Coventry.

Then in 1921 his proudest possession, that Black Cat Café, was smashed to pieces in a riot by unemployed demonstrators who assumed that anyone called Carl Heimann *had* to be German. His café was uninsured.

Over the years he clambered slowly back, until he called the tune in the Palais business that set 10 million feet dancing across the land. Profits came quick-quick—and even quicker—and Mecca stayed with the BBC!

So Carl told his story to me. We edited the film, and he presented one copy to his wife, one to Stuart, and one to the Mecca Organization. Four years later the second heart attack that Carl had feared arrived . . . and killed him.

His memorial remains a personal, private and rarely seen programme; but that was just how he and Stuart wanted it. RIP.

*   *   *

Occasionally, when asked to make such a private

194

or a corporate film, I spend most of the time watching the experts and their creative process. I have filmed in champagne country as often as possible; at Jerez de la Frontera, a delightful setting for significant sherry bodegas. So when invited to go up to Scotland to study Bell's whisky for a while and complete my alcoholic trio, I was fascinated to see how Scotch earned its stars, as I studied a wee dram or two.

Raymond Miquel, then Chairman of Bell's, was a wiry, energetic man who drove his company with a sort of Japanese zeal. He had instilled a strict hierarchy, with senior executives on the road jogging every morning and earning their green blazers, rather like those international golfers.

I had been asked to interview selected members of the workforce, and even given a vague outline of useful questions, so efficient were they. As I started my interview with a group of cellarmen I detected something rather odd was going on. Their answers seemed curiously prescient, though confused. It was some time before I realized they must have been able to forecast what I was going to say, or see in the dark. It was all very strange.

Raymond Miquel was an exacting boss and not prepared to accept vague replies from his staff about work in progress so they had been coached to answer a certain sequence of questions approved by management, and knew exactly what they were supposed to say, and when I was coming.

In fact, they were answering questions I hadn't *asked* yet. I had not found out about their invisible scripts. It was like a *Two Ronnies* sketch, with the Bell's side answering the questions before they were put. I thought we were having a normal chat;

195

they thought it was a prepared inquisition. They were ahead of me, all the time. I just have a memory of total bafflement. We never untangled that one; it was back to base, and start again. I never felt quite the same about *The Two Ronnies*.

*   *   *

There are all sorts of reasons for making films for internal consumption. Some years ago the morale of British Telecom was at a low ebb. A survey had concluded that BT engineers were so ashamed of their reputation they would tell friends they worked for some other company, in a different field.

So an idea was cooked up by Saatchi & Saatchi to give the workforce a new pride in their achievements. A few short films were made to show them just how great they all were.

I had been enlisted for a splendid chore: to go round the world in thirty days with a small crew, marshalled by an intense bearded man, an Account Director from Saatchi's, who at some point had been a speech-writer for Mrs Thatcher but did not long survive his attempt to correct her grammar.

He found frenetic Tokyo disappointing and not at *all* like Japan. No kimonos or cherry blossom . . . only hordes of salarymen streaming in and out of every giant office building. It wasn't until we got to the ancient capital of Kyoto that he glimpsed what he could believe was the *real* Japan.

In Kyoto we set up in a riocan, a traditional inn with tatami floors and clear waterfalls running through the house. A smiling mama-san presented

196

me with a yakarta, and in exchange took my trousers away to be pressed. Our interpreter was a delightful girl from Saatchi's Tokyo office, brought up and educated in America. Aged 26, she was stranded between two cultures, and searching in despair for a Western husband. She told me she was known in Japanese circles as a Christmas cake—that's something everyone wants up until 25 December, but is little valued afterwards . . .

Once made aware of this rejection we saw there were animated 'cakes' everywhere in Tokyo, in every office or café twittering together in girlie flocks, flat little bodies in bright linens and tight jeans. Their lives are Vuitton and Chanel but their ultimate luxury was to spend the night in the privacy of a hotel bedroom, away from the tiny crowded homes they share with their families. It all seemed rather sad and reinforced my view that Japan is a paradise for men, but a confining space for women.

We were staying at the Okura, a splendid, coolly efficient but mildly depressing establishment with gloomy lighting and high ceilings, its vast rooms decorated in shades of brown—the colours of old kimonos. Well, yes . . . but you have to speak in hushed tones. They have since been lightened. At the entrance to the hotel pool a large notice warns: 'No tattoos in pool area'—their way of keeping out the Yakuza, the Japanese Mafia. I preferred the Christmas cakes.

The hotel was the ultimate place to observe a certain level of Japanese life. In the dining room staff bowed low as two middle-aged women left with huge doggy bags of the plainest steamed rice. At another table a particularly unattractive man in

197

his 50s twinkled at a disinterested Christmas cake. His cufflinks were huge diamond flowers with emerald leaves. Half way through the meal he produced a monstrous diamond ring and gave it to the girl. She slipped it on, smiled, took if off and returned it. He put in on his own finger, and then handed it back.

Pass-the-ring was still going on as we left. Was he trying to sell it to her? Or was she saying, 'Get your teeth fixed, find a decent tailor, I need a bigger flat . . .' We shall never know—but it certainly wasn't romantic.

As the man from Saatchi's said, it didn't look at *all* like Japan.

24

I AWAITED THE STRETCHER-BEARERS, BLEEDING QUIETLY

'I say, I say, I say . . . A client goes into his advertising agency and asks an executive, "What time is it?" The exec, pitching for any account, offers: 'What time, sir, would you *like* it to be?"

The offices of advertising agencies are chic, flowers fresh, staff attentive, wine excellent. It's a beguiling parallel universe full of clever, creative people preparing to sell us all the things we never knew we needed. Occasionally I'm invited into this glossy world, to find myself torn between envy, enjoyment and a sort of shock at the indulgence that comes from watching other people's money spent with abandon and flair.

Along the way I've been asked to do many commercials, almost all rejected, though one or two fitted exactly—when I was in some exotic location, say, and couldn't remember whether I was talking to camera for *Whicker's World,* Travelocity, Barclaycard or some other deserving cause.

We had been filming in northern Thailand, in excruciating heat. The unit nurse was much in demand. We were very fortunate that in Phuket the company had taken over the best rooms in a splendid beachside hotel. Our ground-floor suite opened directly on to the sand, and in the still of the mornings we walked the length of the bay in the warm and shallow sea, enjoying a few calm moments before the day's filming.

It was just before Christmas, so the resort was full of holidaymakers. We made the most of our wide French windows which opened onto the sunlit beach, but everyone was anxious to finish the shoot and fly home.

I was rather sad that, agreeable though they were, our crew was not prepared to do some light catch-up work over Christmas, as we used to in the old BBC pre-union days where holidays fitted into the filming schedule. I muttered a few words about the Technicians' Union bosses as we packed. Somehow the place seemed to be holding its breath. After a last swim in that gorgeous bay, we drove to the airport and set off towards the chill and sodden streets of London.

A few days later the tsunami struck. Many of the swimmers drowned and much of the hotel was obliterated. If I had won my argument we might have gone down with the rest of them.

You will now never hear me complain about union rules . . .

The Travelocity scripts we were working on pre-tsunami were so clever I assumed I'd written them myself. So? That was until the second day's shoot, when I narrowly avoided the possibility of sandy suffocation, followed by burial up to the nostrils on a dark beach at midnight—and that was just the start . . .

I liked all the people I was dealing with, I liked their ideas (provided I could walk away from them) and their mildly Pythonesque take on my travels: 'Anyone can be Alan Whicker!' At the advertising industry conference they later won all the awards for some of the sharpest and most entertaining scripts I had read. You won't be surprised to learn that the American organization that owned the company that had triumphed instantly sacked most of their innovative British team.

So their account executive went and got married, closely followed by the product supervisor. Even marriage must have seemed, for the time being, easier and calmer than peddling scripts to product managers around Soho Square. This emptied each winter as ideas men found a good excuse to head for the Cape Town sun where the weather is usually perfect and the extraordinary scenery provides a Chelsea square, a desert, vineyard, mountain and so on . . . all within a radius of a few miles.

Local film crews are amiable, knowledgeable and happily free from strop, if not from proliferation. On *Whicker's World* we travel light and, as far as possible, economically, so the call-sheet for a commercial shoot often comes as a shock. For Travelocity I assumed that as many as a dozen people would be required on location to handle things lavishly. Not quite. We took out a crew of sixty-six or so, joined by three or four times as many locally employed. Fortunately, not my worry.

The two directors were pleasant 40-somethings joined at the hip who finished each other's sentences. They had their own producer and stylist—a delightful man employed to make me look more like me. Then there were the clever creatives, a young, inexperienced couple—she with pink hair, he earnest and balding. Their brief was to make commercials that would hook the lucrative youth market. They did so, with originality. I'm not *quite* sure where I fitted into this, but was too polite and happy with the Cape of Good Hope sunshine to query their selections.

There were also a number of personnel with incomprehensible job titles, all indispensable. Two senior agency directors were on hand, officially to oversee the project, but in truth they just had to keep one Very Important Person happy: the client. She, understandably, loved coming on shoots far from the dreary everyday hassle of her marketing office, so was dazzled, distracted and indulged like a child on a Christmas treat with Granny.

This particular client was a chubby, dark-haired Bridget Jones in her 30s, jolly fodder for the entertaining smoothies from Soho Square who ensured she had the time of her life. While we filmed in sun or rain on midnight beach or empty desert, she was whisked from one Table Mountain to the next until she forgot that somewhere in the small print along the shoot she was actually paying for all the treats and helicopter flights. Seemed to me she was just enjoying a well-deserved break.

In this never-never-land of unreality, even I was treated like royalty—can you wonder nobody had to be asked twice to join such a hard-working jolly? Even my motor-home had a double bed, microwave oven, dining room, air conditioning, television . . . I could scarcely bear to leave it for the turmoil outside.

My every need was anticipated. I was not even allowed to carry my own attaché case, let alone the tripod legs which had haunted my fifty years of being willing, on location.

Any *Whicker's World* is a fast shoot. We aim to catch the essence of someone or something, then move on to the next person, next story, next country. With commercials, of course, endless camera repeats are the norm. Get it right on the first take or—more likely—the second, and the director will nod without much conviction and ask you to repeat it a few more times, looking a shade to the right . . . or was it left?

Everybody knows that a really good commercial needs at least thirty or forty takes of everything. With sixty-six people on that call-sheet, each has a valid opinion and a sensible reaction that needs justification. This is less fun than it sounds when you are trying to breathe through a mouthful of beach.

After about thirty unnecessary takes of one simple shot I distinctly heard the client tell a director, 'He should smile more.' She was later banned from the shoot because, itwas explained, I was rather shy. I wasn't shy, I was going to *kill* her.

My first scene had been in a Japanese restaurant,

whichwas not as simple as it sounded. I was required to lie like a reclining Buddha on a moving sushi bar surrounded by androgynous Asian kids. Wearing pads on my elbows and hips, I edged on and off this moving platform while conversing politely about the product. Around Take 14, I was asked to change the script from sushi to sashimi, doubtless to impress a more aspirational audience. You say sushi, I say sashimi—let's call the whole thing off!

For our next scene we drove an hour or so out of the city to what appeared to be a different country. Huge sand dunes make a convincing desert, and all I had to say in this take was, 'Hello, Morocco!' while in the distance a man led two camels over the crest of a distant dune and said, 'That's Alan Whicker!' The scene is beautiful, but high winds blow sand in horizontal gusts into eyes, hair and equipment. As in *Ice Cold in Alex,* my caravan rocked.

Just after 8 p.m. a message arrived over the horizon: one of the camels was getting the hump. So that's a wrap, and we make our way gratefully back towards the hotel. The truck ahead of us turned sharply as it struggled to climb a dune, and crashed heavily on its side, passengers spilling out. No fatalities.

In addition, now, to black-and-blue our amiable crew are every shade—white through coffee to deepest black. I detect no tension. They all climbed into their favourite bar each evening, when we finished. It seemed a society at peace with itself; but just when you think the old violence has wound up, my driver carefully skirted a scattered township. Unwise, he said, to drive a

Mercedes near *that* lot.

Each day we prepared for the unexpected, which was usually uncomfortable. Smartly dressed, I spent a day in and out of a giant hot jacuzzi. My blazer recovered quite quickly from those sodden hours, but the silk ties will never be the same again.

One day I am on a beach at midnight buried up to my neck, next day stuffed into a giant basket which some poor local had to carry through a vineyard while he picked grapes. My message encouraged travel.

One night I spent six hours squeezed into the drawer of an office desk, reminding me of being decompressed in 1959 at Los Alamos, home of the atom bomb. That wasn't muchfun, either.

We were staying at the famous Mount Nelson Hotel in Cape Town. The Nellie was proud of its Thirties décor and afternoon teas. In our magnificent suite everything was thick and heavily Old Colonial, wonderfully comfortable and like the stage of an opera house. All that plush. Preparing for the usual early call, I climbed out of bed and yanked back the heavily brocaded drapes to unleash that morning's ration of wonderful sunshine into the room. Brocade curtains, pelmet and thick metal rail gave way and crashed down upon my head. It was what's known as a Stunning Blow.

There is blood everywhere, great pools of it. Can't imagine where I kept it all. When I telephoned for help I explained what had happened, assuming that a doctor, a nurse even, would come galloping to the rescue bearing bandages, medicaments and soothing words.

Instead, silence. I waited and waited, and after half an hour there was a tentative knock at the door. Three jolly little housemaids had arrived to resurrect the curtains. The staff knew their priorities.

The maids set about their task, totally unconcerned by my white face amongst the bloody towels and curtains, and my need to hold on to the furniture when I moved. The Mount Nelson continued to show total disinterest in our crisis. I was patched up, not by some caring medic, but by Melissa from Soho Square. She arrived with a small medicine chest for travellers and the information that my car was waiting for me. At £30,000 a day the show must go on, with or without blood.

This distinctive wake-up call had left me reeling about the room in some confusion. What still amazed me was the amount of blood I had been carrying around without complaint. It still dripped from my forehead, down on to much of our extensive suite, soaking bed and furnishings. We telephoned again for help and explained what had happened. Reception was suitably shocked.

Then I sat and waited for the stretcher-bearers, bleeding quietly.

The chambermaids were still worrying about the curtains they had come to replace, which were not at the top of my emergency list. Our director arrived soon afterwards, worrying that I might not make the shoot. I was congratulated by the doctor when he finally joined us, because the scar would be above my hairline and thus invisible to the camera: 'Very professional,' he said, adding that I was not to worry—the shoot would *not* be affected.

During the shoot Wardrobe tried to reorganize my appearance. I was sent for a studio portrait with a plain white background. Since I'd been buried alive and sodden, the dressing-down seemed too late.

I discovered later my face was to be superimposed upon various characters in national dress: a giraffe-necked woman with a neck full of golden rings, a cowboy at a rodeo, a jungle tribesman with long white hair, a Red Indian in war paint, a hunky Australian surfer, an Eskimo with reindeer, and various refugees from the *National Geographic* . . . Made a lovely Christmas card, though!

A few weeks later I saw the images on the biggest billboards in London. Bit overpowering, as I was wearing Britain's modest national dress: a blazer.

The owners of the hotel, the Orient Express, promised me a holiday anywhere in their territory to make amends and apologize for their ropey curtain track, and the fact that hopefully the film company might not sue them for millions to cover their star's injuries, and undertake the complicated re-shoot.

Their holiday invitation never turned up. You don't get much sympathy these days for almost-invisible scars . . . or for the hidden dent in a most delicate skull.

25

A RATHER SMALL UTRILLO

Before Florida became a territory of the United States in 1921, the country was inhabited by Seminole Indians, the scrubby terrain too harsh for all but a handful of white ranchers. A Spanish ship, the *Providencia*, loaded with 20,000 coconuts from Trinidad, was wrecked in the Atlantic, its cargo floating ashore on to an island 14 miles long and half a mile wide—and Palm Beach was born.

Seventy years later the railroad magnate, Henry Flagler, saw an opportunity to create a winter resort for the rich. They could escape the cold of New York and New England for a gentle temperate climate—much as wealthy Europeans chose to winter in the South of France. He purchased 140 acres of deserted shore lined with cabbage palms, built the East Coast railway and the Royal Ponciana Hotel on Lake Worth and, for a privileged few, a new way of life was invented.

When I arrived to make a *Whicker's World* in 1976, Palm Beach seemed like a parallel universe. Manicured and discreet behind high hedges, it had the appearance of a child's model village: no dirt, no weeds, no beggars, no bad people—and definitely no Seminole Indians. Arriving to stay with a friend, I left my car in her driveway. Within an hour, two patrolmen were at the door asking our hostess about this unknown vehicle and the stranger in town. Reassuring, certainly—though faintly alarming.

We were at the peak of the season to take a look at this closed community shielded from reality by money and frivolity. Palm Beach had much in common with Monte Carlo at the turn of the century—instead of La Belle Otero and Edward VII, there was the occasional aristocrat with an obscure title and the ever-competitive society hostesses. For these *grandes dames* of a certain age, the town was their stage and an extravagant charity event the nearest thing to an awards ceremony.

It was said that many of these elegantly dressed society ladies were ex-chorus girls, ex-call girls and ex-hairdressers. Their stepladder to social stardom usually involved several marriages to ever more successful men, gathering fortunes along the way like giant snowballs. Here, it was imperative to have money—lots of it—to be Protestant and, above all, white. Colour was for the hired help whose presence in town after dark was discouraged; they lived across the bridge in West Palm Beach, on another planet.

In the days before people opened their beautiful homes to glossy magazines in return for financial acknowledgement, the lives of the seriously rich were a mystery to all but their friends. Years earlier I had made *Whicker's World*s about Paul Getty, the Duchess of Alba, Baroness Fiona Thyssen—but they were all seen in isolation, in their homes. This was something quite different: a whole town dedicated to the pleasures of living with great wealth. Making money is a proper American occupation, but being seen to spend it correctly is more difficult.

This was the place to come and buy a suitable

home when you had made it elsewhere. Problems in the real world could be left behind because in this never-never-land there was no crime, no poverty, no unpleasant reminders of the real world. Yet the accoutrements of wealth mean nothing without validation—there was a need to be recognized, and to winter in Palm Beach signalled to the world, 'I have arrived.'

This girls' town was a matriarchal society with a pecking order as strict as any Indian caste system. The Brahmins—the old money—were less visible. They belonged to the Bath and Tennis Club and the Everglades, and assumed a quiet elegance away from newer, glitzier residents. They would appear at a gallery opening or chair a committee for some significant fund-raising event, but mostly they kept to themselves and dined in each other's homes, discreetly. Old money had no reason to spend or to be seen. By their names shall you know them. The bathroom billionaires: the life pattern of success being what it is, most of them were widows—Mrs Listerine, Mrs Gillette, Mrs Absorbine, Mrs Q-Tips . . . Among the few surviving bathroom men were then Mr Kleenex and Mr Alka-Seltzer. Mr Borax had got fed up with his title, and left town.

In this land of make-believe it was vital to know your place. Newcomers must never tread on toes. Mrs Mary Sandford, an actress and dancer in another life, then the tough widow of a patrician polo player, was in those days Queen Bee, her attendant princesses fluttering around vying for position and favour. Her beady stare of disapproval was to be avoided at all costs. Committees were formed and money donated, balls organized for the Red Cross, for hospitals, for cancer, for eyes, for obscure animals. All the important causes were allocated to long-term residents. If you were new in town you began at the tail end of the queue raising funds for, say, an animal shelter.

Jews were excluded from membership of the smartest clubs and were not welcome even as guests; inviting Estée Lauder or Leonard Bernstein to a private dinner at the Everglades risked expulsion to the nether world of social Siberia. So the Jewish contingent built their own country club, where the food was infinitely better. As Irish Catholic Democrats, the Kennedy family were greeted with similar disdain. Only the elderly and dignified Rose was treated with respect. It was said that JFK's assassination was cause for celebration in some of Palm Beach's grander homes.

I wandered happily through this social jungle with my cameras. I had the advantage of belonging to an endangered species—a single man in possession of a dinner jacket was much sought after. I had been apprehensive about penetrating those tall hedges but in no time at all we were propelled into a whirl of parties and fashion shows, gossip and confidences. In this Shangri-La, cosmetic surgery was a way of life well before such things became commonplace elsewhere; no one grew old here. Drunks were driven safely home by kindly policemen, dustbins were emptied twice a day; no wonder residents asked each other: 'Where do you live, in real life?'

A jolly afternoon spent with Ann Hamilton, mother of the tanned actor George, gave the Alan

Whicker Appreciation Society their motto: 'How can I lie about my age when my son needs a face lift?' A relatively impecunious man admitted to having 'a rather small Utrillo'. I thought cosmetic surgery might fix it. I had a lot of letters asking me to explain *that* one. The venerable Mrs Betty Battin—known as Mrs IBM because of her happy retention of shares—explained that she had no fear when wearing her considerable jewellery collection as her driver was 'a private detective'.

The only heavy industry in town was art. There were amateur painters galore given fawning attention by gallery owners hoping that after a showing friends of the artist would feel obliged to make a purchase. There were professionals too who were contracted to produce an endless stream of expensive but easily digestible artworks guaranteed not to frighten the horses. And in every home an idealized portrait of the owner beamed down from a dominant position.

To be outside this golden circle was less amusing. Juliette de Marcellus, an attractive musician born and brought up in Palm Beach, told me that as a single woman she was sometimes invited to a lunch, but never, ever, to dinner. The elegant Pam Symes, a sales woman at Gucci, dressed beautifully, buying all her clothes from the Church Mouse—the second-hand shop where expensive cast-offs really had been 'gently worn'.

Somewhere between a carnival and a pantomime, the season danced on until spring, when the caravan moved on to other homes in other states—but nowhere quite as significant . . .

A few months ago I made a return visit for my

Journey of a Lifetime. It was summer. The town was still impeccably kept, but empty. Staying in one of the better hotels out of season felt strange. Restaurants with names like Taboo and The Leopard Lounge were unchanged, though they had a Seventies feel about them. The food was as bad as ever. The Everglades, they told me, had finally admitted Jews . . . but the service had deteriorated. Mar-a-Lago, the grandest house in town, had been turned into an expensive club owned by Donald Trump, his brash style of entertaining leaving the Old Guard transfixed with horror.

Most of the endearing battleaxes of the past were long gone to that great ballroom in the sky, but two of my interviewees were still there, single women living within a few blocks but unknown to each other. Palm Beach, they explained, was like the inside of a watch: many little wheels turning around, none of them touching each other. The golfers didn't mix with the art crowd, the old residents deplored the new and there were no queens or princesses any more.

Times had changed. People ate carefully and did not drink; 10 p.m. had become the Palm Beach midnight—everyone needed to be home to watch the late-night news, and there were no more drunks needing to be tucked up in bed.

A few new grand houses had been built by speculators—'McMansions', Juliette de Marcellus called them—faux grand with plastic windows. The first Russians had arrived, paying $100 million for the most expensive property ever sold in Palm Beach. The new money was, as ever, regarded with suspicion. 'Nobody knows where it comes from—

at least before we knew, because we used all their products . . . Kleenex, Q-Tips, Borax. Now who are these people? They come here with their trophy wives—models or actresses—but they don't stay long. Once they've done their shopping on Worth Avenue they find there is nothing for them to do and no one to impress. It's all a big disappointment.'

Society photographers used to have a certain power—women felt forced to buy their prints for fear of seeing an unflattering photograph published as a sort of reprimand in the *Shiny Sheet,* the local paper so named for the quality of newsprint specially chosen not to blacken delicate fingers. Now, they told me, readers were no longer interested in society women. Gossip columns were hungry only for the exploits of Hollywood actresses and better-known celebrities. Palm Beach could no longer compete with the young and beautiful.

Some things, though, had not changed. Visiting an old Palm Beach friend with my pretty 27-year-old producer, our hostess looked at her and exclaimed: 'My dear, you're beautiful, but you must have your portrait painted. Do it *now*, before it's too late . . .'

26

THIRTY BODYGUARDS FOR DINNER

The Year of Spain was going to be 1992. Madrid would be European Capital of Culture, Expo was launching in Seville, the Olympics were planned for Barcelona. Everything was happening—or to be precise, as this was Spain not a *lot* was happening.

There is something infuriating but charming about a national state of complete disorganization. It was quite clear to the most casual onlooker that nothing would be finished on time—and then, somehow, all is snatched from total lethargy at the very last moment and everyone smiles, as though living on the edge of chaos was perfectly natural and you shouldn't be alarmed by such impeccable organization.

I had filmed in Spain a few times. *Matador,* with El Cordobés, was the first bullfight seen on British television. At home it stirred a frenzy of fury and delight. Then there were those few frustrating weeks with the Duchess of Alba, head of an impossibly aristocratic family with sixty-eight significant titles. This meant that were she a man she could have worn her hat in the presence of the King.

I had also enjoyed social visits with winemakers and sherry barons, but now I was being asked by the BBC to explore modern Spain eighteen years after the death of Franco, to try and make sense of this vast jigsaw of a country.

It was as though Spain had been asleep during the thirty-six years of rigid authoritarian repression and, on awakening, had thrown off the covers and danced through the streets. There was a hunger to live all the lives that had been denied by the old regime, in the shortest possible time.

Yet, conversely, in certain parts of the country life could be feudal, an interesting mix of tradition and hedonism. For the first time I realized that here was a collection of states with nothing much in common but a name. Still, better to be offered multiple personalities than no personality at all . . .

You arrive in Spain before you board the plane at Heathrow. With no complications and no other passengers in sight, it can still take a good fifteen minutes to check in; the girl shrugs and smiles in a good-natured way and you hope you'll see your case again; somehow, it seems unlikely.

On arrival a sense of joyful anarchy seems rampant. In the early Nineties there had been 300 per cent inflation over four years, but the black economy reigned and kept everything moving. Income tax was 56 per cent and wealth tax 86 per cent—but there was a distinct impression that most people didn't take the notion of tax too seriously. A company in Barcelona supplied false VAT invoices to businessmen to enable them to launder their money at home—a facility advertised in local papers.

In this *laissez-faire* atmosphere fortunes were being made. 'If you can't make money under this Socialist government,' I was told, 'you must be very stupid.' But with such instant prosperity came danger. The law, which in Franco's day was total and severe, was now disregarded and a sort of joke. No one paid much attention to the police, and drugs flooded in across open borders. Dealing was a criminal offence, but possession for personal use was legal.

For muggers in the roughest districts of Madrid the weapon of choice was a syringe full of AIDS-contaminated blood, a dreadful threat. Any motorist neglecting to remove the radio from his parked car did not expect to see it again. In Seville it was unwise to stop at a red light, when the boot could be ransacked, a windscreen smashed.

For the rich there was a constant fear of kidnap from ETA, the Basque separatist movement. ETA, I was told, were not interested in *Hello!* people who might possibly be famous, but only in the seriously wealthy. They seemed to have inside knowledge about top earners, so it would appear that a lot of extremely rich people paid a protection tax to be left alone. The terrorists were known to be completely ruthless, kidnapping businessmen and, if no ransom were paid, killing without compunction.

Dining in the splendid Zalacain restaurant one night, I saw the Minister of Justice being entertained by a well-known entrepreneur. They each had five bodyguards on duty, and seemed to regard such attention as money well spent. When the King or his father chose to visit that restaurant I was told there would be some thirty protection officers on duty, with a helicopter flying overhead. This did not seem to interfere with the meal.

Everyone was relaxed. Elegant women strolled along elegant streets—smoking, of course—and wearing the kind of exotic fur coats that would have been paint-bombed in Knightsbridge within

216

five minutes. The siesta was still a way of life and there was as much traffic on the streets at 3 a.m. as at 3 p.m. No one in Madrid ever said, 'Can't have another drink, I'm driving,' or, 'Sorry, I have to work in the morning.' Barcelona may be Europe, they told me proudly, but Madrid is still Spain.

I stayed in the Ritz, an island of calm and good taste with starched linen sheets and the kind of housemaids now only seen in pre-war Hollywood films. I half expected to meet Marlene or Greta Garbo gliding across the lobby—unlikely, as the Ritz considered itself an unofficial annex to the Royal Palace and discouraged 'rogues and vagabonds' from the acting profession who might encourage some trend as vulgar as publicity.

In this sea of disorder most people still lived lives of conformity. Working in a sort of superior PR job at the hotel was a well-connected young aristocrat, an attractive divorcee with a young daughter. The long and difficult process of divorce was only legalized in 1981. After Mariola divorced her alcoholic husband she was shunned as a traitor to her background, her class and her religion. Former friends would walk past her in the street. She was a social outcast.

This gentle, dignified young woman was rejected for making a choice commonplace in every Western society, but she had broken the code. Here was an example of the paradox of Spain: a light froth of modernity disguising deep roots of tradition.

I visited Aline, Countess of Romanones, an American heiress with a racy background in wartime intelligence. Slim and impeccably dressed, she looked more like the perfect hostess than a trained killer. I found it hard to believe that this fragile creature could deal a mean karate chop. Instead, I asked about her friend, Ava Gardner. 'Quite impossible,' she said. 'I had her to a dinner with the Windsors and she got bored, went off to a nightclub without a word and took my butler with her.' If she had not taken the hired help, it's just possible she might have been invited again.

To explore traditional Spain I drove down to Andalucia and found myself alone on an hotel balcony in Arcos de la Frontera, contemplating spectacular views of rolling fields and hills stretching to the horizon. It was like being on an aircraft—only the pilot was missing. My promised guide was nowhere to be seen. I had forgotten that all itineraries in Spain come with a built-in glitch. A few hours later she arrived in a panic, a dizzy 22-year-old blonde with a basket full of cakes by way of a peace offering. She proved surprisingly efficient—and the cakes were delicious.

My first call was to the Duchess of Medina Sidonia, known as the Red Duchess, famous for her outspoken opposition to Franco and her flaming red hair.

Threading through the tiny winding streets we arrived at a vast palace. A butler let us in through a side door and I followed him up an ancient staircase into a stuffy office where a tiny, wizened woman was working on a computer. I assumed she was an elderly secretary and that the sizzling temptress would emerge from some inner sanctum—but no, this was indeed our Duchess.

She was tiny, bright-eyed and febrile, the custodian of an extraordinary archive reaching back to the 12th century. There were piles of letters from Columbus, eye-witness accounts of the Battle of Trafalgar. Her files, she said, would alter the received history of Spain. Passionate and paranoid, she believed she was about to be arrested and her archive sequestered.

A gang of unfriendly dachshunds gnashed their teeth as she explained that the Socialist government wished to rewrite history and that her treasure-trove belonged to the world. I left full of admiration for this feisty Miss Haversham, but with the disloyal feeling that maybe such precious manuscripts would be safer elsewhere.

They say that to be comfortable in Jerez de la Frontera you need to be a Domecq, or a horse. The family dominated the sherry industry while remaining closer to the soil, some of them breeding bulls, another raising beautiful Andalucian horses. Don José Ignacio Domecq Jr was a lean, leathery, polo-playing cigar smoker looking like a Jilly Cooper hero in his perfectly cut tweed jacket. We made polite conversation as we toured his remarkable vineyards but I saw a different, animated man emerge when we reached the stables. There was no doubt where his heart lay.

Later I met his father, José Ignacio Sr, known as the Grand Old Man of sherry, and famous for his enormous nose. This skinny little man wearing an ugly tie, a shirt too big for him and an ill-fitting suit somehow contrived to have enormous charm and presence. King of all he surveyed, he worked in a scruffy little office inches deep in dog hairs. He travelled around on an ancient red motorbike, a box on the back for Paco, the Jack Russell. A member of Opus Dei, he worshipped in church three times a day, played a mean game of polo and smoked heavily despite having to preserve the most respected nose in Jerez.

Wine-makers the world over have a relaxed, happy outlook, and the sherry-makers of Jerez with their warm hospitality and courtly good manners were exceptional. It was clear that certain aspects of life had not changed over the centuries, but the fear of an unsympathetic Socialist government was sending faint tremors of alarm among the famous names. Land was being confiscated, new rules and regulations emerging to curb their influence and, worst of all, Middle England had lost its taste for sherry, their delicious product with its many varieties.

There was one man who appeared to bridge the gap between the old and the new: Ambassador Prado, the King's financial advisor and fixer-in-chief. He was a twinkly one-armed aristocrat descended from Christopher Columbus, who lived in spectacular grandeur on a vast estate near Aracena. Photographs of him sailing and shooting with the royal family were sprinkled throughout the house. On the afternoon we met he had just returned from a private audience with the King. Small, intense and magnetic, he was seen to be the power behind the throne and author of the new Constitution. This, I thought, must be the face of modern Spain.

Days later he invited me to an extraordinary party. Unable to attend El Rocio, Andalucia's annual bacchanalia where a million pilgrims pile into ox carts and spend five days and nights dancing, drinking and singing, he decided to recreate the spectacle at home on his own 3,000 acres.

First there was Holy Communion celebrated on a hillside with soft gypsy guitars and pipe music, women sitting on the grass in flamenco dresses like flocks of multicoloured butterflies. After lunch in a decorated Moroccan tent, a famous bullfighter started to dance flamenco on the grass, all eyes and hips, bucolic and sensual.

Soon everyone joined in, except those intruders from the real world, the dark-suited bodyguards watchful behind their shades. If I still wanted to find the new streamlined ultra-modern Spain, I would have to look elsewhere.

27

THE RIGHT INTERESTS: LADIES, HORSE-RACING—AND TAKING THE LOCALS FOR A RIDE

I once saw James Hanson dining with Audrey Hepburn at the Ritz. I think it was the only time in my life I've ever felt a twinge of jealousy. She was gorgeous, he was handsome and rich—and they were engaged. Later, as I watched their Bentley glide away towards Belgravia I realized there was an argument for being born into a Yorkshire trucking business, in Huddersfield.

Years later, when I became part of a syndicate that won the Yorkshire Television franchise, it became apparent that our delightful bunch of local landowners and worthies had little knowledge of my business: television. At dinner with our new

Chairman I mentioned that I was leaving for Brazil next day. 'In coffee, are you?' he asked. I said Yes, I was . . .

It was a relief when James, by now the extraordinarily successful entrepreneur behind the Hanson Trust, came on board. His business partner and surrogate brother was Gordon White, another tall Yorkshireman with a flair for business and a sharp eye for pretty women and expensive horses.

They were almost telepathic in their closeness, and their ever-expanding interests on both sides of the Atlantic covered everything from brick-making and garden tools to fishing fleets and sausages. In the exuberance of the Thatcher years it seemed the Hanson Trust could do no wrong.

In 1985 I filmed a BBC series about America as seen through the eyes of British immigrants. So many dreams and expectations were invested in this hunt for a better life somewhere else. The possibilities were limitless and the constrictions of history or habit could be discarded like an old skin—a new life emerging as easily as running in a new set of tyres. Reasons for leaving were as varied as Tolstoy's unhappy families, but the common thread was the search for a future that promises an intangible trophy somewhere just over the horizon.

In the years of the Callaghan government, with Denis Healey threatening to squeeze the rich until the pips squeaked, Gordon White decided to move to New York. He could hardly be described as an economic migrant, having already accumulated a considerable fortune in London, but the heavy hand of the Labour government was a dead weight on his entrepreneurial spirit. Along with Jimmy Goldsmith and a handful of others, he took off for New York and—operating out of a twentieth-floor think tank on Park—never looked back.

Gordon had been expelled from school at 16 (he set fire to the place) and became a wartime pilot flying clandestine operations for SOE in the Far East. Diffident and slightly deaf, he'd broken his neck on the Cresta, and the odd few bones on the hunting field. An unlikely tycoon, he hid his sharp business acumen under a veil of flirtatious good humour. Happier chatting to girls than talking to bankers, he used his playboy reputation to his advantage. Always competitive, he had adapted easily to flying his own helicopter and was proud of completing his training long before younger classmates.

Part Peter Pan, part gentleman pirate, he had left his home in London in 1973 to perch in a Carlyle hotel suite with his American friend Eddie Collins. He was 50, his only assets a fat address book and $3,000—the maximum currency allowed out of Britain in the days of exchange control. Nobody knew who he was and no one cared. Luckily he had never believed that New York's streets were paved with gold.

Gordon had a complex attitude towards the Britain he had left behind, and combined a fierce hatred of the 1970s political atmosphere with a romanticized vision of home. He despised his narrow-minded Yorkshire roots while never attempting to lose a slight North Country accent. However transatlantic his lifestyle and ambitions, he felt very British. He was in America to win, and to put British interests back on the map. He hated

New York winters but knew they provided his spiritual home. 'If you live here, you feel you can conquer the world.' A huge painting of the Battle of Trafalgar hung behind his office desk.

He was lanky and soft-spoken, and it was easy for the US business community to dismiss him as a lightweight, more at home in the gossip columns than the *Financial Times,* yet he became the most successful British financial buccaneer in America. 'You have to count your fingers after you've done a deal with Gordy,' one notoriously touchy US businessman told me, ruefully. Socially he wore his responsibilities so lightly his friends asked me, 'Does he *ever* do any work?'

He certainly did work, but without an entourage. He was a solitary who walked from his Park Avenue apartment to his office every morning with the trusty Eddie, and ate lunch each day at the same Italian restaurant. He succeeded on Wall Street where most Englishmen fail because he grasped early on that doing business in Wall Street had little in common with the City of London.

'Whenever you feel the warm, comforting arm of some American businessman around your shoulder, you soon feel the pain as the knife goes in! They only understand excellence in this country. You cannot get by with mediocrity— which you still can in England.'

The mistake most of his contemporaries made when they did business in New York was to believe they were talking to another Englishman with a funny accent, so 90 per cent of their efforts ended in failure. 'The Brits didn't understand that the thinking process, the work ethos, even the stamina was different; business people here are ruthless and trained to work very hard.'

He also understood the way political patronage could affect every aspect of life in his adopted country. 'You can't fiddle around with an institution at home—but here, if you've been nice to the Mayor when he's looking for some campaign contributions, then he might intervene for you with a judge and help you on your way. Provide him with money up-front for his election, that's a campaign contribution. Give him money once he's been elected, that's a bribe.'

The Hanson strategy was to snap up companies with a strong cash flow but weak or bloated management. He and James looked for stable companies in basic, unexciting industries which they could strip down to the essentials, often selling off the unwanted parts of the business for as much as they had paid for the whole company.

Gordon was the thinker, the strategist; he was imaginative but cautious. 'My father told me that any fool could sell but it takes a clever man to buy. I suppose I can see when something is the right price. If you buy at the right price you're not going to make a mistake. The problem that most people make coming over here is that they pay too much. When I look at an acquisition I never look at how much we can make, I'm only interested in what we might lose.'

He was totally uninterested in the management of the companies he took over, never visiting their factories. 'I don't believe in royal visits.' Balance-sheets were his bedtime reading. His adrenaline fix was in the thrill of the chase. He left the nitty-gritty of management to James Hanson. 'I speak to Gordon five or six times a day,' James told me,

225

'but he doesn't always let me know what he's doing.'

He reserved his anger for lawyers whom he believed to be parasites, whose only purpose was to prolong and complicate any deal in order to earn more fees for themselves. Dealing with the American legal system was a learning process; the urge to sue being second nature in the business community. 'They're throwing out 6,000 lawyers a year, they follow ambulances looking for anyone who's been hit by a car. I've got 185 lawsuits outstanding,' he said. 'Do you sleep nights?' I wondered. 'Of course,' he said. 'Most of them are garbage.

'I've got one to settle now: a black man working in one of our depots had a lady supervisor. She couldn't get on with him, and one morning when she came in he was in the loo, so she went along looking underneath the doors, and when she could see his feet she banged on the door. It wasn't locked, he jumped to his feet—and she fired him for indecent exposure!

'So he sued the company for a million dollars for sexual harassment! We offered him another job, we offered to move her—in the end we settled for $7,500. You have to settle. It's very expensive to fight a legal battle. It's all part of the process of doing business in New York.'

Gordon had his own idiosyncratic style of negotiation. Walking alone into a room full of lawyers and advisers he would lounge about and tell jokes, pretending not to understand what was happening, lulling his opponents into a false sense of security. He called it 'being low key'. He knew the value of what he was buying or selling, and

226

bargaining bored him. He was happy to shake hands with the other side and leave the room within minutes if he felt they weren't ready to make a deal. Yet I can't believe this dumb-bunny act convinced *too* many people!

Notwithstanding all his achievements, there was a vulnerability about Gordon. At the time of our interview he was on his third tour as a bachelor, those endless balance-sheets having driven his second wife away. The clothes in his dressing room hung neat and colour coded, but his beautifully decorated apartment felt empty.

One night he heard I was going to a small dinner for Anna Wintour, Editor of *Vogue*, and asked if he could come too. The predatory women of New York were not really his style and there was a temporary hiatus in his love life.

Another weekend I flew to LA with him in his company 1–11. The warmth and the casual lifestyle relaxed him and we were surrounded by showbiz cronies and pretty girls. On the return journey he disappeared into the back cabin with a Charlie's Angel and closed the door before take-off to shouts of 'This is not the Mile High Club, it's the Two Foot Six Club.' His playboy reputation was intact. He was *still* taking the locals (feminine) for a ride.

Some months later I was filming in Beverly Hills and had lunch with Gordon at the beautiful ranch house he was renting for the winter. The other guest was Elizabeth Taylor, who was, of course, late. She was about to make a brief cameo appearance in some film and was on a serious diet—she ate only a plateful of fruit. Gordon, ever sensitive to weight gain, had once confided that if

227

his trousers felt even the slightest bit tight he simply stopped eating until they felt comfortable again.

'I wonder,' whispered Gordon, 'if you'd mind asking to see that interview you did with me, on video? I'd like Elizabeth to see it.' As they were both free at the time, I thought he was up to his old tricks again. But no, he said he couldn't deal with the complications of such a liaison. They'd been to the ballet together a few nights before—she was late as usual and the performance in the Opera House had been held up until she arrived. He didn't think he could cope with American royalty on a regular basis.

Later, after seeing Gordon's interview on *Whicker's World,* a famous publisher sensed that there was a book in Gordon. Knowing his susceptibility to a pretty girl, the publisher sent his most attractive ghost writer to the Hanson office. Gordon liked the girl and liked the idea. 'But how much are you going to pay me for this book?' he asked.

The publisher, who believed it was a vanity project, was rather taken aback and offered a low advance. 'You've got to be joking,' said Gordon . . . The project never got off the ground.

A Yorkshire businessman has his price—though he didn't charge *us* for this interview!

28

BACKSTAGE AT THE ROYAL PALACE

We arrive at Bandar Seri Begawan, Brunei's tiny capital, a little after midnight. It was a long journey from Jersey. We are a motley group, even non-drinkers clutching duty frees in preparation for weeks in this newly dry outpost in South-East Asia. There is our *Whicker's World* camera crew with director David Green; a team of polo players; Major Christopher Hanbury, the Sultan's jolly man-about-London; a flock of gentlemanly Asprey salesmen; various wives, girlfriends and a smooth operator who says he is the Sultan's art consultant.

Only the outline of the floodlit Royal Palace glimmers in the darkness, a sprawling building shaped like a huge Noah's Ark. It is said to be the largest building in the world created for domestic use. Our handlers emphasize, rather defensively, that it is also the seat of government, which is confusing since the Sultan *is* the government and most of the ministers are his relations. Anyhow, it has 1,778 rooms, which settles most arguments.

In the morning light we appreciate for the first time the reality of Brunei. It may be the richest small country in the world—but it is no phantasmagoria, no Dubai or Abu Dhabi. The Sheraton Utama is all too real. Then the most modern hotel in the country, serviceable but uninviting, more Holiday Inn than Mandarin Oriental. It soon became apparent that this was a sort of up-market bazaar; everyone had something to sell.

Around a small swimming pool the merchants of the world lay pale-skinned and tense, ears strained for the magic call that would summon them to The Presence to tempt him with goodies from afar, with jewels, cars, aircraft, anything that might interest a man who need never deny himself anything. All the right names are here: Cartier, Van Cleef, Rolls-Royce, Boeing, British Aerospace, as well as the chancers and con men, each hoping for that once-in-a-lifetime deal—like Billy Bunter expecting his tuck box.

The coffee shop is filled with forlorn men resigned to hanging about for weeks on end in this international waiting room. Time did not exactly stand still, but clocks appeared to run on Brunei time, which was whatever the Sultan wanted it to be.

The polo players had been flown in specially to play the Sultan's team, and had to make sure the visitors didn't win. They had no idea when their match might be—perhaps Saturday or possibly next week. The art consultant, who had no gallery and did not appear to be attached to anyone, told us that his client had a wonderful eye for pictures. Of course.

The top two floors of the hotel are given over to an unusual collection of people working for the various royal families. One girl is kept on permanent standby from six in the morning until nine at night—she teaches the royal children dancing and is usually called upon twice a day. A young couple talk to no one and appear only after dark like bright-eyed bush babies when they step into an anonymous limousine and head off into the night.

We are told that they are fitness instructors for Prince Jefri, the playboy prince who, apparently, doesn't *do* mornings. In fact, he doesn't do daytime much at all. People whisper about his extravagance: gifts, girls, cars—and much else. If only a fraction of the gossip is true, sleepy Brunei has a secret life like something out of *A Thousand and One Nights.*

Old hands who are familiar with the nocturnal habits of certain members of the Sultan's extended family prepare themselves for the out-of-office-hours house-calls that may lie ahead. Two world-weary dentists, regular commuters from London, always spend a restful night in Singapore so they can arrive drill-fresh and ready for any 4 a.m. call. Keeping people waiting may be a national pastime, but it is a one-sided game. An Aspreys wife complains that her husband is frequently woken in the small hours by some minor princeling enquiring whether his watch is ready. Time-keeping is not a strong point around here.

HM, as they call him, is charming, helpful, smiling and uncertain. He worries about how he might be perceived on television when his English is not up to scratch. Here, in his own country, he lives in a diamond-encrusted cage isolated by birth and position from all except his own family—small wonder that he views a visit into *Whicker's World* with some apprehension.

I ask if we can film him flying his plane or his chopper, playing tennis, doing something he enjoys. He smiles encouragement and says, 'We'll see.' Later I discover this is polite Brunei-speak for 'No'.

231

This bashful billionaire was not experienced at answering questions: 'I *never* give interviews,' he told me. Certainly none of his courtiers or his people would dare ask him anything. Handsome, laughing easily, disarmingly shy, he seemed to have no hidden depths. Indeed I found it surprising that an absolute monarch could remain so balanced and sensible and, you could say, ordinary . . .

HM is small, muscular and boyish with greying hair—indeed one of our points of contact was that we shared a barber. More significantly, we were both Bentley enthusiasts who preferred two-door coach-built models.

A good solid basis, you may think, for a relationship, but unfortunately our similarities diverged quite noticeably when we began marching to a different income. The annual expenditure of the Sultan, his brothers and their families had been estimated at well over £1bn.

One of the occupational hazards of being such a monarch, I reflected as we considered opening his closed world to the ultimate intrusion of television, was that he must suffer the inevitable disturbance of reality that comes from having too much money and too little to spend it on. If he can think of it, he can *have* it. With expenditure limited only by imagination he can do or buy or control anything he wants, and with that sort of power surely never hears the word 'No'; but how many palaces, cars, ponies, diamonds, airliners . . . can he cope with?

A rich man's jokes are always funny, so he's surrounded by a lot of hearty laughter. Everyone who meets an absolute monarch sells out, in a way.

At our first meeting we had one of those amiable conversations which drift along pleasantly—but afterwards you're not quite sure what has been achieved, if anything.

We had to adjust quite quickly to the fact that in Brunei—the size of Norfolk but richer than Australia—the Sultan was no longer just a dashing youngish fellow behind the smoked glass of a souped-up white Mini Cooper vrooming happily round and round Hyde Park Corner. No longer just the slight, elusive figure slipping through the Dorchester lobby about whom the assistant manager told me thoughtfully, 'The Sultan? Oh he's a nice little fellow—no trouble at all . . .'

Back at the Brunei hotel we are asked not to speak to other guests. If the word gets around that we have breached the palace walls we will find ourselves with a lot of new best friends clinging to our coat-tails in the hope of getting a toe through that golden door.

We have a drink with the Asprey people. They are favoured visitors to the various palaces and much envied by other salesmen. Their rooms are piled high with trunks that will travel back to London empty, ready for the next onslaught in a few weeks' time. On this battlefront you don't have to wait too long to find out you're a loser.

'I don't want to sell him anything,' I explained to a member of the Brunei royal set, 'I just want to make him as big as Ginger Rogers.' There was a sort of joke in there somewhere, but his expression didn't change.

Acquisition is one of the few acceptable diversions, and a trusted salesman soon becomes a palace pet. These palaces, they say, are whispering chambers; if the Sultan makes a joke it will be repeated instantly and heard back seven times within the hour. It's *The King and I* meets the Ottoman Empire, all the luxuries of the 21st-century while stepping firmly back into the past. Brunei women lack freedom and choice here; one young royal cousin asks wistfully about such treasured and secret glamour: 'Have you ever been . . . to *Boots?*'

So we have islands of hope and excitement surrounded by oceans of boredom and irritation. We are used to filling every moment of the working day, but here we sit like Cartier salesmen waiting for the call that sometimes comes but usually doesn't. The sultry energy-sapping heat is dispiriting. We have seen the splendid new mosque with its golden dome, toured the water village with its houses on stilts, visited the dusty department store with its rails of tiny padded bras.

In desperation we plan a boat trip down river to see the Iban tribesmen in their picturesque longhouses. As we get ready for this expedition an official from some unidentified ministry arrives and announces that the Iban are a backward people and will not show Brunei in a progressive light, so we are not to film them. A day later we are escorted to a newly constructed model longhouse which meets government approval. It could be on a housing estate in Milton Keynes.

On one of these tours of inspection, whenever the Sultan spotted us trailing him he would come up cheerfully and say, 'How are you? Enjoying the place? Now we're going on to a school. I hope you enjoy it . . .' He always seemed most concerned. We had a lot of this happy enthusiasm until I suddenly realized that the Sultan thought this momentary exchange of cheerful chat was an interview! I heard him telling Christopher Hanbury, 'We've done lots of interviews all over the place.' It was hard to convince him that we hadn't travelled around the world three times for a chat about the weather, however charming.

So we follow the Sultan around on his inspection tours. He is engaging, attractive, smiling, but the candid and relaxed interview we hope for is elusive. To fill in the time we talk to ex-pats and visit their homes. Some have lived here for years, watching the country change from an unimportant dot on the map to a land with enough economic power to shock the world's markets.

One couple and their six children live in happy chaos on the edge of the rainforest in a ramshackle bungalow, a remnant of times past. The mother, an orphaned gibbon slung around her neck, talked nostalgically about the Sultan's father, a friendly anglophile who drove a London black cab around his capital, sometimes dropping in for a casual lunch. A part-time teacher, she found her pupils passive, unresponsive and quite unable to grasp the concept of money. Most children would have been enchanted by the tiny monkey that clung to her, but these were terrified.

Other schoolteachers lived in a grand apartment block owned by the Sultan's second wife, Queen Mariam, a former air hostess. Locals had declined to lease this expensive accommodation so the Ministry of Education had been ordered to take over the building and install their employees. The teachers lived happily in subsidized luxury with golf and sailing nearby, a far cry from their previous posts in Zambia or Libya.

The downside was the changing mood within the

country, as Islamic fundamentalists grew steadily more powerful. Every week some new and petty restriction was imposed: the Lions and Rotary Clubs denounced as part of a Zionist conspiracy, amateur dramatics from Shakespeare to Noël Coward censored and cut, anything foreign subject to forensic investigation by the religious police— all silly and easy to ridicule, but slightly sinister to live with.

Corruption had become the accepted currency, oiling the wheels of government. The Sultan, affable but easily bored, preferred to turn a blind eye and avoid confrontation, particularly in matters concerning his own family. No one wanted to give him bad news, fearing not the Sultan himself but the cabal of courtiers surrounding him. It was said that his secretary and gatekeeper owned 200 cars. In the overheated atmosphere of palace politics nobody questioned whence they came.

In all we made three visits to Brunei over a period of several months. We ate endless plates of Brunei noodles, drank a great deal of special tea— beer served from teapots and drunk from thick mugs in Chinese restaurants—and did a lot of waiting around doing not very much.

The Sultan, invariably polite but always remote and shy, gave me an interview of sorts, but nothing like the informal, relaxed conversation I had hoped for—during which he would have been at his best. Vaguely dissatisfied, we were making desultory plans when a sparkling new Mercedes with an even more sparkling driver arrived carrying an invitation to be HM's personal guests at the various celebrations planned for his Silver

Jubilee. With an official car we were transformed and seen to have been smiled upon from On High, and were treated with new deference. Our handlers, a rather sour bunch who previously smiled only when the conversation turned to Manchester United, suddenly became unctuous and helpful.

The Throne Room was a vast golden cavern with huge chandeliers, its centrepiece an extraordinary gold pagoda under a golden canopy—everything blindingly gold. We were still on Brunei time, which meant a wait of two and a half hours while the room filled with local dignitaries dressed in traditional silks of black and gold. Later the Sultans and Sultanas of various Malaysian states arrived, turbans ablaze with diamonds. Then HM appeared with his two wives dressed like identical twins in elaborate robes, one in silver, one in gold. It was a Cecil B. DeMille fantasy crossed with a 19th-century Durbar.

Later the Sultan was dragged through the streets in the State Coach, a curious-looking vehicle somewhere between an elongated chariot and Cleopatra's barge, a scream of army and police motorcycles surrounding him. Crowds lined the route, strangely quiet, unresponsive and low-key. I suspected it would be deemed disrespectful to show enthusiasm.

Our transmission was timed to coincide with HM's state visit to Britain, and I was invited to a discreet Foreign Office lunch in his honour. There were about thirty of us seated at a vast table. As the Sultan arrived accompanied by his first wife draped with the mandatory ropes of diamonds, the earnest American woman beside me asked breathlessly, 'Do you think they're *real?*' Quite obviously she had never been to Brunei.

Not to be out-blinged, our own Queen arrived for the Brunei state dinner glittering in thumbnail-sized emeralds from her personal collection. Even the visiting royals were impressed.

It is some seventeen years since I made my programme on *The Absolute Monarch.* The Sultan is no longer the richest man in the world. He had to make way for all those American supermarket owners and internet people. He was as good as his word and never did give another interview. Brunei has faded from view, emerging occasionally onto the news pages following some scandalous high-profile court cases usually involving his brother, Prince Jefri.

The Sultan remains so royal, so elevated, so protected by court protocol that it still feels like trying to reach God for a chat. However, he remains a charming deity who, despite his power, is almost diffident—though his subjects, from hereditary noblemen to rainforest tribesmen, fall silent and abashed in his presence.

To reach him is never easy. Once we had moved through endless protective barriers and finally reached the Godhead, the Sultan was always open, friendly, and indeed rather jolly. One day he was seen brandishing a copy of my autobiography, *Within Whicker's World.* It was open at a photograph of a heterosexual group getting closely acquainted in a jacuzzi at Plato's Sex Club in Beverly Hills. The Sultan whispered conspiratorially to Christopher Hanbury, 'Which one is Mr Whicker?'

No one could accuse their capital Bandar of

being stimulating or offering many distractions. There can be few duller places in the world. Though only two or three flying hours from the thrust of Singapore or the excitement of Bangkok, it feels like an indolent colonial outpost without parliament or political parties, discos or bars, bookshops or concert halls . . .

Until 1950 and the arrival of oil, the old palace was on stilts in the harbour. Now the Sultan's main home is in the Istana Nurul Iman, the world's largest private residence, several times grander than Buckingham Palace. This Sultan-sized palace has a floor space of more than 50 acres. It is not cosy.

There I met the Sultan's representative in London, Pengiran Data Setia Yusof Sepiudein, a diplomat who learned to stand and wait during a year spent working in the dining room of Blake's Hotel, SW7. He lived near Marble Arch but lost much of his enthusiasm for London when his wife was mugged at knifepoint. Despite this he planned to retire to Cheshire, or maybe Eastbourne.

Another asset to Brunei, Major Christopher Hanbury, had broken his leg in three places playing polo—as one does—so the Sultan sent his private secretary to show us where he could be interviewed, in due course. We walked through chambers full of presents celebrating his Silver Jubilee. The most insignificant item I noted was a small rock crystal flask thinly trimmed around its middle with gold, rubies and emeralds—evidently some afterthought duty-gift from which no one could even be bothered to remove the jeweller's price tag: £59,500. That's thousands.

Queen Mariam, the Sultan's second wife, had

been discovered by the Brunei religious police in a compromising situation, compelling the Sultan to divorce her. She now lives quietly in London on his generous allowance, and indulges in her favourite occupation: gambling.

In one of London's smarter casinos she met an attractive young croupier. He is now driving a Bentley and teaching the ex-Queen to play golf. She is very happy.

On this state visit the Sultan was met at Victoria Station by the Queen and Prince Philip, and stayed with them at Buckingham Palace for a few days. He lunched at No. 10 with Prime Minister John Major and the Lord Mayor before completing this holiday in his own mansion among 47 acres of Southall, Middlesex.

The Sultan's magnificent banquet honouring our royal family on this State occasion was held at his Dorchester Hotel amid banks of orchids said to have cost £250,000, which mesmerized the Queen.

Some 55 per cent of all possible viewers watched our Brunei television programme, *The Absolute Monarch*, which was then shown around the world. The Sultan enjoyed it, he said. Our Queen was also most generous.

Prince Jefri had ordered half-a-dozen BMWs to be air-freighted out to Brunei with gold ignition keys and left gift-wrapped outside his friends' homes. He also spent £3.2 million on ten watches set with jewels showing a couple copulating every hour on the hour. We all celebrate birthdays in our chosen ways.

A dignified messenger arrived delivering a bulky gift from His Majesty. We held our breath. Within a massive velour box lined with royal yellow satin

240

was a small yellow plate showing the Sultan's portrait.

At least it was Spode.

During the scintillating preparation for the royal event my cameraman wanted to see how the Throne Room looked when its massive array of lights were shining. Click—it's *brilliant!* Pop—all the lights have fused. They then had to change 800 ceiling bulbs before dawn.

As we leave I thanked the Sultan's amusing secretary for his guidance and concern. 'That's all right,' he said. 'I'll bill you.'

29

NEVER A FRIENDLY ARMOURED DIVISION AROUND WHEN YOU NEED ONE

I awoke in Verona. There were no signs of violence. Our billet, which I had taken over the day before, had been occupied by Germany's State Secret Police, the Sicherheitspolizei. They were surprisingly clean and tidy, I'll say that for them, though you might not care for their interrogations. At least they left none of the frightening vibes that emanated from former Gestapo buildings I had visited, which were still oppressed by the screams of earlier occupants.

My radio announced that the German forces in Italy had been cut in two, and the capture and liberation of Verona 'was expected soon'. This was disconcerting as I had been living in Verona for several days. They might have told me I was liable to be shot on sight, deliberately.

Now in its final stages, the war was disintegrating. I had been commanding the Army Film and Photo Unit since the Eighth Army had landed in Sicily to create a second front on 10 July 1943. We had fought our way up through Cassino and the Anzio bridgehead, then Rome and through the Apennines and down into the Po Valley. Scattered surviving German forces were deciding how and where to surrender, but were still armed and anxious to shoot any Allied soldier who was getting too triumphant and casual, just to even things up.

I had taken over this grand villa in Verona so that my cameramen, who operated out in the field, could find a centre while we prepared to go back to army headquarters, wherever that was, and then, hopefully, to Civvy Street.

Most of us by then should have got through the mountains and into the Po Valley. It seemed to me that the Eighth Army must have turned right after capturing Padua and Venice. The Fifth had probably driven towards Turin, and the Fiat factories.

Impatient with the Eighth Army—or maybe it was the Fifth—I was ready to be recruited or liberated by *any* army at that stage of the war, so I filled my elegant 'liberated' Fiat coupé with petrol and rations and headed for Milan, the biggest city available, to look for a few friendly uniforms.

I drove cautiously along the *autostrada*, giving some worried thoughts to mines, but that splendid road seemed clear. There was no movement at all.

I had not seen an army—ours or theirs—for several days. It seemed that the enemy had gone, and *we* had not arrived. Yet somewhere within this silent ominous landscape a fearful war was ending. That seemed the most reassuring sit-rep, so I chose to believe it.

After a few diversions for blown bridges, I reached the suburbs of Milan without even seeing a German, or being shot at. That was already an improvement. I drove on cautiously through the shuttered streets of the vast city into its very heart, the Piazza del Duomo, and the cathedral. The Milanese began building this magnificent Gothic monument with thirty-five spires in 1386, and completed it in 1813. Italians have always been relaxed about their work schedules.

Now the piazza was empty and silent. I seemed to have captured Milan without anyone noticing. It was like one of those ominous end-of-the-world films; I was the last man alive. As I was taking my first pictures the calm was abruptly shattered by a bunch of partisans with flags and a lot of guns. They noticed me, stopped agitating and shouting and watched me thoughtfully.

I decided that, even if they were Mussolini's anti-Allied Blackshirts, they must have heard about the end of the war, so would have more profitable enterprises to consider—like looting. Having evidently made a similar decision, they tumbled into the piazza and made towards me, still shouting and wanting to shake hands. I was no longer the last man alive.

It seemed they were indeed a partisan group, and had just surrounded the headquarters of Hitler's SS in a hotel in the Via Manzoni, the avenue running from the Duomo towards La Scala, the most famous opera house in the world.

This was a very big catch indeed, though I did not think I could cope with it alone.

The SS had announced they would only surrender to an Allied officer, not to partisans. So far, it appeared I was the only acceptable officer in town. Hence my popularity.

The SS were the special police force founded by Hitler as his personal bodyguard back in 1925, at the start of it all. As the Nazi war machine grew in size they began to provide personnel for the German security services, including the Gestapo and the administration of its concentration camps. Despite those nightmare roles, the Schutzstaffel regarded itself as an elite. The SS were feared and loathed, even within the German armed forces. Tough and skilled, they believed they made the law.

I had been looking for pictures, not prisoners— and especially not massed SS prisoners even if they were ready to surrender. In the distance I could hear where the trouble was: an Italian crowd working up its bloodlust and growing hysterical. The centre of Milan was rapidly changing from deserted to jammed. Any Milanese brave enough to face the uncertainty of the streets was converging upon this last warlike outburst, to be in at the kill—or at the loot.

A large corner building was ringed by layers of high barbed-wire barriers on wooden frames. These held back a mass of jeering Italians. Behind the defensive wall stood scores of silent SS men with automatics, a finger on every trigger. Bigger guns were sticking out of most upstairs windows.

These disciplined troopers ready for an outburst of fire were facing an ugly lynching. They regarded me impassively. There must have been a couple of hundred of them, well armed and disciplined. Behind the wire were a growing number of Milanese holding a surprisingly large armoury of elderly hunting rifles. Hard to tell whether these Italians saw me as saviour or a reckless idiot.

Until now the SS had been running the show. People stepped off the pavement before them. Now they were preparing to go down fighting in a suicidal last stand, taking with them as many Milanese as could be shot in the time available.

Facing them through the barbed wire was a crush of hysterical Italians, not quite sure which side they were on, but giving voice to their opinion of the Allies, with gestures. I seemed to be in the middle of a hateful situation. The enemy was mainly a raggle-taggle of slightly hysterical partisans anxious to prove themselves in what looked like the last hurrah of German resistance in Italy.

I paused for a long moment outside the barbed wire. Then, taking advantage of the quietening mob, I took out my Smith & Wesson .38, and cocked it. It was surprisingly audible and reassuring, and sounded the business.

I thought: I must remember to put the safety catch on afterwards—if there *is* an afterwards. The silent, disciplined SS, facing a lynching, suddenly realized I might have a useful role—like saving their lives.

Pushing aside my sense of survival and accepting a future as a possible SS hostage, I strode past the nonplussed German guard-posts, through the barricades and into the lobby. An elegant SS General in a black uniform stood up. I could sense

245

he was politely concealing disappointment at my lowly rank, but I suspect he thought I was the best Allied officer he was going to get. He clicked his heels, saluted and handed me his revolver. I noticed it was a Walther, several times more effective than my army-issue Smith & Wesson.

'My men are at your disposal,' he said, in English. 'We could not surrender to that . . . *rabble*.' Scornful gesture at the surrounding clamour. He sounded like a country-house hero playing charades, but I could understand his reluctance to surrender. Once disarmed, his men would surely have been shot or, more likely, torn to pieces. In this furious stand-off there was nothing between the hated SS and the partisans— except me with my puny .38, now reinforced by the General's more effective Walther but still, in this atmosphere, insignificant armoury. I regretted I had never learned to fire with both hands, like Hollywood heroes.

Anyhow, I was now committed. I could attempt to dealwith the tumult of jeers and threats facing the menace of SS automatic weapons . . . or walk away on tiptoe and ignore a devastating eruption of Italian rage and revenge—a final bloody massacre in the streets.

All I had in support was the limited authority of three pips on a British battledress and a growing determination not to be pushed around by the heel-clicking remnant of an army we had just beaten in a fair fight, or by a jeering mob loosely controlled by foolhardy but doubtless brave anti-German street fighters.

Acting the stern victor, I told the General that the local uproar must be ignored, difficult though it would be; that any shooting by his men would now be seen as a war crime, and duly punished. I briefly considered telling him to disarm his officers and men and leave their armament in the lobby. A moment's reflection, and this seemed impractical; I could hardly push my way through the growing crowd around the hotel to count their weapons, and once in that mob would doubtless never be seen again.

I expected American armour to arrive at any moment; I told the SS General, when the Italian crowd would be dispersed and he and his men escorted into captivity. I had no idea of course that any of this would actually *happen,* but with so many guns waving about on both sides of the wire it seemed sensible to reassure everyone about everything.

There's never a friendly armoured division around when you need one.

Much fury and loathing seethed in that street, for in the past year some very bad things had been done in Italy by the German occupiers—mainly by the SS and the Gestapo. The massacre of 345 hostages in the Ardeatine caves near Rome was a recent horror.

The screaming had now calmed down a little, so I decided it would be tactically sensible to go outside the hotel occasionally and display myself as a British authority in command. I moved through the barbed wire so the mob could see some progress: one Allied officer, at least, was taking an interest. I repeated this authoritative play-acting a few times during the afternoon, looking stern and hoping it might relieve pressure and prevent some enraged hothead deciding that

247

any Italian mob in good voice could take on a building full of SS machine-gunners, if it was angry enough.

Looking back from the relative security of today, it seems too much to hope that a lone and youthful captain could ever consider trying to control a frenzied Italian horde, while at the same time accepting the surrender of a highly professional unit of German SS anxious to avoid being lynched. Yet war and rank bring instant maturity and authority. In the army orders are obeyed—it is quite unthinkable that they would not be obeyed.

All I had planned to do that morning was to take a few relaxed pictures of the cathedral and perhaps the arrival of the first British troops. Now I was presiding over the last stand of Hitler's killers, who still seemed prepared to die for the Führer.

As though I did not have enough to worry about, at that moment the impeccable SS adjutant came downstairs, followed by two of his men struggling with a heavy tin trunk which they handled as though full of dynamite. I allowed myself to be drawn into a corner of the lobby to watch him unlock it. Then I understood why they were so tense.

It must have been the treasury of the SS in Italy for it was crammed to the brim with every type of currency, filed in precise Germanic order. Piles of familiar lire, sterling and dollars, of course—all big notes, and much of it counterfeit, no doubt, but who's asking? There were Swiss francs and Reichsmarks, pesetas and krona and a lot of crisp exotic notes with portraits I did not recognize. I had never seen so much varied currency in one place, and never have since.

Having ensured that I understood our transaction, the adjutant locked and secured those many millions, handed me the key with a half-smile, saluted and withdrew. His war was over. Mine was not—though at least it seemed to be growing more interesting.

It occurred to me in a happy flash that what I *ought* to do in the middle of all this disorganized panic and confusion was to accept my remarkable luck and order some German soldiers to place Aladdin's trunk in my unmarked Fiat, for safety. This was a legitimate spoil of war, surrendered to me by the enemy. Then at a suitable moment during the evening's chaos I would make my excuses and drive south, back through our lines to the villa outside Florence where I had stayed with my Italian friends.

They would look after it for a year or two, no questions asked. When the wartime dust had settled, I would return and, like Ali Baba, open it and set about becoming very rich indeed. If I did not accept my good luck, somebody else certainly would.

The partisans would still be trying to get at the SS, who would be keeping a finger on every trigger. Then after several hours of noisy confusion during which I held the growing mob at bay and untruthfully assured an increasingly nervous SS commander that I had his surrender well under control, a US tank regiment *did* arrive to liberate Milan, to my surprise and delight.

In the late afternoon, attracted by the constant tumult in our street, several Sherman tanks of the US 1st Armoured Division clattered to a halt outside the hotel, just as I had promised. At the sight of so much serious armour and so many soldiers, the Italian crowd calmed down and the SS began hesitantly to pile its automatics in the hotel lobby, as ordered.

Then, having made the decision of a lifetime, I handed my priceless trunk and key over to the tank commander, along with my German General and all my SS men. They were about to be prisoners, briefly, while I was about to be demobbed and looking for a job.

I returned wearily to taking the pictures of the Duomo and the British and Allied troops that I had neglected during my brief but pivotal role amid the ruins of Hitler's crumbling empire. I already felt nostalgic for my disappearing treasure. It had the comforting quality of a good travelling companion.

There was still one Briton to be caught—the Italian Lord Haw-Haw, treacherous English voice of Italian radio. John Amery was the brother of Julian and son of Leopold Amery, Cabinet Minister and then Secretary of State for India. I went to Milan Radio and told them to broadcast an announcement demanding Amery's whereabouts. Someone instantly called in to say that he was being held by partisans in a city jail. I drove over with Sgt Huggett and told the prison governor to produce him.

'Thank God you're here,' said a very pale Amery when led into the governor's office with his girlfriend, an appealing French brunette in a black trouser suit. 'I thought they were going to shoot me.' His relief was premature. He was, like the hated original Lord Haw-Haw, William Joyce, a candidate for judicial murder.

Amery, small, dark and unshaven, but still wearing the black shirt which proclaimed his political sympathies, told me, 'You can read the scripts of my broadcasts through the years and you'll never find anything against Britain. I've just been very anti-Communist, and if at the moment I'm proved wrong, one of these days you'll find out I was right.'

I took him from his partisan jailors to his great relief, and handed him over to our Military Police. He was later repatriated to Britain and at the Old Bailey stood trial for treason. To save his family further humiliation, Amery pleaded guilty, was convicted and hanged by Albert Pierrepoint.

As he went to the gallows, Amery told the famous hangman, 'I've always hoped to meet you—though not of course under *these* circumstances . . .'

While all this was happening, the Italian dictator Benito Mussolini was preparing for the end of his war at the Villa Feltrinelli on Lago di Garda. He had packed a few gold bars—as you do—with some letters from Churchill and a machine gun, and set off with his German escort to escape to Switzerland or, if he felt like it, to fight to the death in the Italian Alps.

The stolen gold of Dongo was never found, after enquiries ranging up to the Padua Palace of Justice and lasting years. The grubby hands of partisan power had faced my two choices over that trunk full of currency—and made the *other* one. Italian partisans were believed to have seized an estimated $90 million in gold and the 'Treasure of Dongo' was said to include three sacks of wedding rings contributed by Italian servicemen's wives to

251

Mussolini's Ethiopian campaign.

The commander of Mussolini's Blackshirts, one Alessandro Pavolini, had told the Duce he'd bring 3,000 of his best men for a last stand in the mountains. Mussolini decided he liked the idea of fighting to the death amid Alpine thunder and lightning—it would be an operatic climax to his life.

But as they were all about to leave for their final suicidal battle, Pavolini finally came clean and admitted that he only had a dozen men—the other 2,988 had gone home!

Mussolini and his mistress, the gallant Clara Petacci, were executed next morning by a tall, pallid bookkeeper whose name was Walter Audisio. Mussolini even told his Communist killer where he should be shot.

'Shoot me here,' he said, moving his lapel, 'in the chest.' Those were his final words. He died giving orders, as you might expect of a dictator.

Clara died simply, poor lady—almost eagerly.

After killing them, Audisio executed another fifteen of the Duce's few remaining loyal ministers, along with his secretary and pilot. Their bodies were all taken to Milan and before a howling mob strung up like sides of beef outside a garage in the Piazzale Loreto.

It is charitable to believe that Clara's countrymen would not have wished her to die in that way, but given the temper of the times and the vicious mob hysteria she may well have been spared an even worse fate.

Churchill saw the photographs of the final scene and was profoundly shocked by 'this treacherous and cowardly murder'. He took time to send a telegram to Field Marshal Alexander, commanding the Allied forces in Italy, demanding, 'Was she on the list of war criminals? Had Audisio authority from *anyone* to shoot this woman? It seems to me the cleansing hand of British military power should make enquiries on these points.'

30

**THE PARTY'S OVER—
IT'S TIME TO CALL IT A DAY**

It was the sort of rain that only falls in Asia: not benevolent at all. Ugly downpours with sheets of water that drench in seconds and squelch back out of your shoes. This is June 1997, the last week of British rule in Hong Kong. I am here to witness the disappearance of the last significant red dot of Empire. I flew here, not in a professional capacity but because after all these years it seemed right and respectful to be part of this sad moment.

My first visit to the colony was as a war correspondent in 1951, to cover the Korean War. It then took four days to reach Tokyo from London Airport. While our Argonaut refuelled in Hong Kong we all came ashore to have a motionless dinner at the Peninsula, as I relished my last good meal for months.

During the past fifty years I have returned many times to this Oriental crossroads on my way to everywhere, first when still in Fleet Street, then for television. I would come to meet friends or change planes or just to enjoy life in this extraordinary metropolis. It's always hard to constrict this floating Manhattan into an island, yet it remains one of the magnificent settings of the world.

I have watched its changing skyline as apartment blocks began creeping up through the Mid-Levels towards the Peak, and witnessed authority shifting away from the old colonial clubs and Hongs to the new breed of mainland entrepreneurs. Almost unnoticed, Hong Kong has become a symbol of the new world order as power moved East.

In the lobby of the Mandarin I ran into Sir Clement Freud, now sadly no longer with us. He had been a friend since 1968 when we both wrote columns for the *News of the World*, of all papers. He had been summoned to speak in Hong Kong by that strange and significant organization, the Ladies Recreation Club. Most offshores support a smart literary club, usually so in demand that tickets are at a premium. Clay Freud, who spoke with total confidence, would be a popular offering and well worth his fee and his fare from London.

We retreated to the bar, where he told me he was addressing the massed ladies at lunch tomorrow, and suggested I attend. I regretted I was already spoken for, but would get a full report from friends.

By the time we had reached the second round, Clay had relaxed enough to tell me his latest joke. This was, without exception, the dirtiest joke I had ever heard. I looked around guiltily in case Valerie was passing and might have heard some of the scabrous details. 'I hope you're not going to tell that disgusting story to the Hong Kong ladies?' 'I most certainly am,' he said. 'Why do you need to upset their well-balanced applecart?' I asked. 'The club's been running for 114 years—do you want it shut down and off the air before the Handover?' I left him to stun any friends he still had with his exceptionally obscene joke.

Next day was typical Freud. A friend who was at the lunch told me when Clay got to his feet he announced he had a new and very funny story for them. 'I'm hesitating about it, but Alan Whicker *insisted* I tell it to you.'

The story was received in stunned silence. Then a number of members recovered and walked out, each of them doubtless about to hunt me down demanding I apologize or leave the colony. There's friendship for you.

*   *   *

There is excitement and anticipation as well as uncertainty and anxiety at this time of Handover. Will this be a great celebration or another wet weekend? Among the items on our itinerary for the next five days will be competing firework displays from the British and the Chinese, and a ten-hour extravaganza for 60,000 ethnic minorities and foreign domestic workers in Kowloon Park, with the promise of an evening of songs from Amelita Ramos, wife of President Fidel Ramos of the Philippines. We may not be able to squeeze this event into our busy schedule, as they say.

So many familiar faces have already left Hong Kong to flash their new passports around Australia and Canada, Belize and Paraguay and the multitude of obscure places willing to sell passports to the affluent or the nervous, or anyone uncertain about life under new masters. But do

255

you really want to be a citizen of Nauru? Boat people and freedom swimmers—refugees a generation ago—encourage their children to leave, fearful that history may repeat itself.

Others who fled from China in fear towards a protective Union Jack now discover an ancient pride in their heritage and the potential of the newly rich mainland.

Young itinerant Brits, most of them working in finance and known as 'The Filth' (Failed in London, Try Hong Kong), had traditionally cut their business teeth in the old Hongs, and prospered until they suddenly found themselves no longer welcome at the top table in the former colony, their jobs taken by eager Chinese who will not drink much in the pubs, play golf or take long lunch hours.

The island is jammed to capacity for this passing of the torch. I am sleeping in a modest-standard room in the Mandarin, inch by inch probably the most expensive ever, for a week—and lucky to get it.

Will hordes of mainland soldiers now suddenly appear overnight on the streets to impress us, one way or another? On each visit we have observed the small, almost imperceptible changes we were awaiting. Immaculate service has grown a little less immaculate, there are fewer fluent English speakers, and raucous Brits who could commandeer a grill room here, a clipper lounge there, have been replaced by dark-suited mainland Chinese who don't shout much.

Invited for lunch at the Peninsula on its thirtieth floor, I am joined by a sodden Simon Winchester, so dripping wet that the hotel has presented him

256

with a new shirt, and the brilliant Jan Morris. James Morris, as he then was, climbed as far as the Advance Base Camp on Mount Everest to ensure that *The Times* carried the first announcement of the victorious ascent, to be revealed on Coronation Day in 1953. We are part of a diminishing tribe of foreign correspondents, so this will be one of the last memories of shared experiences and laughter.

Simon's latest book is about an English eccentric, one of whose idiosyncrasies was to cut off his own penis. You might think it would be difficult to find a sophisticated group capable of discussing such a subject over lunch with cool urbanity, especially since one of those present actually *did* have his penis cut off and was evidently not too concerned by the conundrum; but it was still no everyday topic.

After lunch we crossed the harbour one last time on the good old Star Ferry and returned to find the Mandarin lobby in a state of suppressed excitement. PR girls with great bunches of flowers prepare to curtsy, managers are already standing to attention, journalists and their editors agog: Lady Thatcher (for it is she) arrives impeccable after her flight from London looking slightly older and slightly bowed, as well she might. Those Iron Butterfly wings that beat against the mighty intransigence of the Beijing regime to so little effect are just a forgiven memory.

Back in my room there are messages from old friends: Stefanie Powers, whom I managed to wake by mistake at dawn, Len Evans, the wine man from Sydney and Rothbury, and the inescapably jolly David Tang. There are parties everywhere, some welcoming the new order, others saying a nostalgic goodbye. I look in on the Foreign Correspondents' Club, that unprepossessing building at the top of Lower Albert Street. Years ago they told me that it was 'a great place for a fight on a Saturday night', though my own memories are predictably of great company and so-so food.

Old colleagues have always gathered here, the charmer Donald Wise, Dick Hughes, who conjured up more reality than there was for the rest of us, Clare Hollingsworth, the oldest resident who watched the Wehrmacht cross the border into Poland, Gavin Lyle taking a slow boat from China, the Far Eastern correspondent of the *Telegraph* who sailed down the river to rescue his stringer from Vietnam with the help of Lee Kwan Yew. They're not making correspondents like that these days.

Amidst the glitz of downtown Hong Kong there was always a breath of old reality here, though who knows how long it will last as newspapers dispense with journalists and budgets are cut. In the age of the internet the foreign correspondent is doomed, along with his expense account. RIP.

Instead—as it is now Saturday—we have a splendid but uneasy Chinese meal with our old friends Gerald and Cecily Godfrey. Distracted and cool, they seem ready to pounce on any perceived criticism of the new regime. As in most divorces, friends take sides, and these two, it seems, have already made their choice. All the old warmth has gone as they snipe at each other throughout the meal. What used to be amusing banter is now tiresome and embarrassing. She, who was a funny lady, is now permanently cross and violently anti-

British, a little concentrated ball of Korean fury. This is disconcerting and rather alarming. There is a strong feeling that we *gweilos*—'white ghosts', the Chinese call us—have a past from which they need to distance themselves, publicly and urgently.

As a long-established white ghost I have already watched some of my Hong Kong Chinese friends returning to their heritage at the Happy Valley race track. I gave them a last bow, and my understanding. Being unfashionable to some groups is not at all fatal, I observed. Indeed, if you *must* know, I hardly noticed that most of them had gone and left me!

Time passes in a haze of lunches and dinners. There is a spectacular night with David English, Managing Director of the *Daily Mail* and of Associated Press and saviour of the Rothermere family fortunes. He has invited Nick Lloyd, Eve Pollard and Anne Leslie. We have a meal in a restaurant on the thirty-fifth floor overlooking the harbour, an endless stream of cars nose to tail beneath us inching towards Central. Afterwards we stand on the roof and watch this illuminated procession and consider that in two days' time this majestic and beautiful place will be handed over to the Chinese. Later we return to our hotel, go to the bar, and get down to some serious correspondents' chat. We finish around 3.30 a.m., so it must have been a satisfactory night. There won't be many more . . .

One day before the big event and David Tang is giving a dinner at the China Club. Valerie is to be seated between Dominic Lawson and Max Hastings, then editors of the *Sunday Telegraph* and the *Evening Standard*. She findsthe prospect of dinner between two heavyweights rather daunting. David English whispers to her: 'You can runrings round both of them,' and she thinks it the most flattering accolade she has ever received. In fact David is absolutely right.

I am next to Chantal Miller, wife of the amazingly wealthy Bob who owns most duty frees, and the mother of three gorgeous girls who've all married into serious royalty. She was born in Quito, Ecuador. Attractive in a highly polished way, she talks about her various homes. I ask if she has anything in England and she tries to remember: Yes, a sort of shooting lodge . . . Turns out to be an entire Yorkshire village.

Later I talk to Patten's aide, who has been by his side for these eventful years. He is about to sail into the UK sunset on *Britannia* and then head for his next posting, in Bosnia. That's a reward?

Monday 30 June—the reason why this disparate group of people have come together. I am still not quite sure what has drawn each of us back here. Is it the last sentence of the last chapter of a story that really ended fifty years ago, a way of life that staggered on with one foot in the traditions of another century, the other foot far into the future . . . ?

We watch the Pattens leave Government House. Pipers play, police escort, tears flow—it is very emotional. The previous morning we had listened to a radio phone-in when weeping callers thanked the Governor for what he had attempted to do. Contrary to reports from a HK business community anxious about its future relationships with its new masters, it appears that he and his appealing family reached out to touch far more people than was ever expected.

In the evening another deluge—like a biblical plague without the frogs. The dignitaries take their seats for the ceremony and we watch, smugly dry with wide screens in the Mandarin. Water drips off the nose of the Prince of Wales as the flag is lowered. Everyone is cold and wet. Women rush to cloakrooms to wring out sodden underwear . . . This is the auspicious beginning of the new era?

We climb onto the roof of the Mandarin with Trevor McDonald and the ITN crew to watch *Britannia* sail. The Royal Yacht moves away, escorted by the frigate *Chatham.* The lights are beautiful. It is a tranquil end to a strange, damp day.

I am starting to write this book, in my mind. On an adjacent rooftop a party of raucous Brits are blasting out 'Rule Britannia'. Below us a Chinese crowd are cheering China and listening to Jackie Chan—who's not singing, just shouting into a mike.

The King is dead, long live Somebody . . .

ACKNOWLEDGEMENTS

My thanks to David Green, Stan Griffin and Katharine Begg, who starred in this memorial journey, and to Jonathan Taylor for publishing guidance.

Gratitude as always to Jack Gold and Mike Tuchner, who were there at the beginning and were joined by the late Fred Burnley and by my *Tonight* and Yorkshire TV friends for more than half a century of action and memories.

And thanks to Laureen and Sarah Fraser, who keep my working life running smoothly.